Microwave Cooking My Way
It's a Matter of Time

Microwave Cooking

my way

IT'S A MATTER OF TIME

 **By Grace Wheeler**

Rand Editions
San Diego

Pictured on the cover:

Crab Stuffed Chicken Breasts, page 56
Parslied Rice, page 104
Fresh Vegetable Medley, page 92
Caribbean Pineapple Upside-Down Cake, page 161

Cover photos courtesy of SAN DIEGO HOME/GARDEN Magazine.

Library of Congress Catalog Card Number 80-53591
ISBN 0-914488-25-2

Editor: Elizabeth Rand
Illustrator: Marian Telleson

First edition of *Microwave Cooking My Way* published May 1978
by Grace Wheeler.

This book is dedicated to my family — to my husband and to my children who participated in the perfection of these recipes, and who endured all of the experimentation and tasting experiences.

A special thanks to the many people in my life who stimulated and encouraged me to compile this collection of my recipes.

Contents

Thoughts on Microwave Cooking

Microwave cooking is fun and an interesting way to cook! In some respects it is challenging, even though the microwave is a very simple unit to use. Because of its speed and method of cooking you must rearrange your thoughts. The size of most microwave ovens is limiting, so the order in which you are going to do things for your meal preparation becomes important.

Cooking with a microwave oven offers many advantages besides speed. Convenience, simplicity, and ease of cleaning are some of its attributes. Generally, you will save half to three-quarters of the conventional cooking time, and the microwave uses less energy than conventional cooking. Also, it does not heat up the kitchen.

Be adventuresome; experiment and try many microwave recipes as well as your own favorites. Use your microwave to its fullest! By doing so you can, if you desire, use it for about 90 percent of your cooking needs. It will do much more than the ordinary appliance, but you do have to realize it has its limitations.

Microwave cooking differs from conventional cooking in that there is no radiated heat involved. It is a vibration or excitement of moisture molecules creating heat. With most microwave ovens you are now cooking with time alone, rather than with temperature *and* time as in conventional cooking.

Timing becomes very important!

Microwaves pass through non-metal utensils without heating them. In some cases, because of the heat involved, heat transfer from the food to the utensil causes heat to be felt—in most instances, however, not enough to require the use of hot pads.

Many paper products may be used in microwave cooking—another advantage, as then you can throw the cooking utensil away and eliminate some dishwashing. Plastic containers as well as plastic wrap and bags may also be used.

Cooking in the same dish you are going to serve from, or eat out of, ultimately saves you dishwashing, energy and time.

All the recipes in this book have been converted or created by me; they have been tested and perfected using the dish size and method I feel give the greatest satisfaction as to the end result. If you vary the ingredients or dish size from those given, you may have to alter the timing.

As you try the recipes you'll find "My Way" may differ from the instructions given in other microwave cookbooks. Keep in mind that personal preference is still involved in microwave cooking as in any other form of cooking. Also, foods will vary in size and shape, and because of this you may have to adjust cooking times (see MORE FOOD FOR THOUGHT, page 214).

Each microwave oven differs in its cooking pattern and speed. Voltage and wattage variations will cause differences also. The recipes in this book were tested in an oven with a 650-watt output. If your oven has a higher wattage, cooking times will be less. If it has a lower output, you will have to increase the cooking time. For further specific information regarding the use of your own oven, refer to your owner's manual and keep those instructions in mind.

With the thought that all microwave ovens do not have a variable power feature, high or full power is used for most of the recipes in this book. A lower power setting, however, has been incorporated in some recipes and will be indicated when used.

Most important to remember and consider in microwave cooking is the density of the food, the amount or volume of food being cooked, and the beginning temperature of ingredients in a recipe. Then . . . "It's a Matter of Time!"

Grace

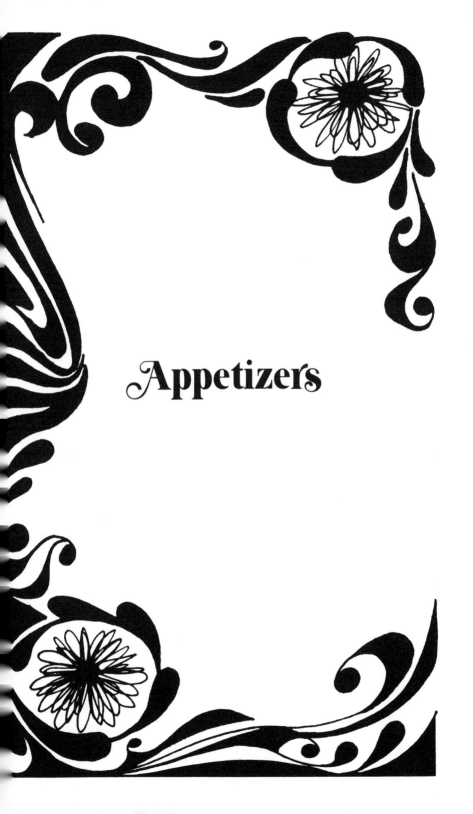

Appetizers

APPETIZERS

Appetizers, party foods, hors d'oeuvre—whatever you call them —are often the foods guests like most. A party serving only hors d'oeuvre, with various beverages, of course, and a finale of desserts and coffee, is one of my favorite ways of entertaining. With the microwave oven, a large variety of appetizers can be made without spending hours in the kitchen. The following recipes include some that can be frozen or refrigerated, as well as some of the last-minute variety. All are favorites of mine. I hope they will be yours too.

FOOD FOR THOUGHT:

Don't forget to include thinly sliced roast beef or ham (prepared in the microwave, of course) along with small rounds of various breads, and mustards and relishes for that extra-hearty hors d'oeuvre when needed.

* * * * * * * * * *

Plastic meat trays make excellent freezing and reheating containers for appetizers.

12

Artichoke Frittata

A unique finger food with an Italian flavor.

    1   can (14 oz.) artichoke hearts
    1   bunch green onions (about 6)
    2   Tbl. olive oil
    4   eggs
    1   tsp. salt
    ⅛   tsp. cayenne
    1   clove garlic finely minced or ⅛ tsp. garlic powder
    1   cup (4 oz.) grated cheddar cheese
    1   Tbl. chopped fresh parsley
    ¼   cup fine dry Italian seasoned bread crumbs
         Paprika

Drain artichokes and chop fine. Set aside. Chop the green onions including tops; place in a small bowl with the olive oil. Cook 1 minute 30 seconds. In a large bowl beat the eggs well with the salt, cayenne and garlic; add the chopped artichokes, sautéed green onions, cheese, parsley, and bread crumbs. Pour into a lightly greased 6 × 10-inch glass baking dish that has 1 Tbl. dry bread crumbs sprinkled on the bottom. Sprinkle Frittata lightly with paprika; microwave covered with wax paper about 8 minutes 30 seconds or until firm to the touch and a knife comes out clean when inserted in the center. Let stand 5 minutes before cutting into squares. Serve warm or at room temperature.

FOOD FOR THOUGHT:

Place Frittata squares in paper bonbon cases for easier serving; arrange on serving plate garnished with fresh parsley sprigs. A nice touch!

Italian seasoned bread crumbs are available in most grocery stores; if not, use plain bread crumbs, 2 Tbl. Parmesan cheese and 1 tsp. Italian seasonings, crushed.

Appetizer Cheesecake Squares

Crust:

½ cup margarine
1¼ cup flour, unsifted
⅛ tsp. garlic powder
¼ tsp. salt
1 Tbl. Parmesan cheese

Soften margarine (about 30 seconds). Blend in flour, garlic powder, salt and Parmesan cheese. Press dough into a lightly greased 6 × 10-inch glass utility dish. Cook about 4 minutes or until firm. Set aside to cool while making filling.

Filling:

1 package (8 oz.) cream cheese
1 egg
½ tsp. *each* salt and Worcestershire sauce
1 Tbl. lemon juice
⅛ tsp. cayenne
1 Tbl. flour
½ cup *each* finely chopped green pepper, onion, and celery

Topping:

½ to ¾ cup sour cream
¼ tsp. *each* salt and Worcestershire sauce
Stuffed green or ripe olives, cut in rings, or fresh minced parsley for garnish

In a glass bowl soften cream cheese (about 15 to 30 seconds). Always remove foil wrapper first! Beat until smooth. Blend in remaining filling ingredients. Pour evenly over baked crust. Cook 5 to 6 minutes. Rotate dish 3 times during cooking. Meanwhile, combine sour cream, salt, and Worcestershire sauce; spread evenly over filling and cook 1 minute longer.

Cool slightly and place sliced olive rings over top, spacing 1 inch apart, or sprinkle overall with minced parsley. Cut into squares while warm. Chill well before removing from dish. If difficult to remove from dish, heat a wet towel on the microwave about 25 seconds or until quite warm, place dish on it for a few minutes.

Makes about 60 one-inch squares.

FOOD FOR THOUGHT:

For a nice effect when serving, place squares in paper bonbon cases before arranging on your serving plate. Garnish with fresh parsley.

Bonbon cases are similar to paper cupcake liners, only in miniature.

Cheddar Shortbread

Good as an appetizer or with soup or salad.

½	cup butter or margarine
1	cup (4 oz.) shredded cheddar cheese
1½	cups flour, unsifted
½	tsp. salt
⅛	tsp. cayenne
1 to 2	Tbl. minced onion, optional
	Paprika or chili powder

In a large bowl suitable for the microwave, soften the butter or margarine (this will take about 30 seconds). Mix in the cheese; stir in the flour, salt, cayenne and onion. Knead lightly to blend well. Press evenly into a lightly greased 6 × 10-inch utility dish. Sprinkle top lightly with paprika or chili powder. Cook on full power 6 to 7 minutes or until firm and no longer doughy. While hot, cut into bars or squares with a sharp knife. Let cool slightly before removing from dish. Serve warm or cold.

Makes 40 1¼-inch squares.

For variation:

Add 2 Tbl. sesame or poppy seed to the dough. Sprinkle top with an additional tablespoon of either seed, pressing in lightly with finger tips.

Bacon bits also make a tasty addition!

Chicken Cashew Appetizers

Nut-crusted bites of chicken.

2	chicken breasts, split, skinned and boned
¼	cup cornstarch
½	tsp. each salt and sugar
⅛	tsp. garlic powder or 1 small clove garlic, minced fine
2	egg whites slightly beaten
2	Tbl. vermouth or brandy
1½	cups (6½ oz.) salted cashews, finely chopped

Cut chicken breasts into 1-inch cubes. Combine cornstarch, sugar, salt and garlic. Stir in beaten egg whites, brandy or vermouth. Spear chicken cube with a toothpick and dip in egg white mixture, roll in chopped nuts. Place on a suitable serving dish that can be used in the microwave oven. For even cooking place larger pieces to the outside edge of the plate. Cook covered with paper toweling 4 minutes 30 seconds to 5 minutes.

Makes 35 to 40 pieces.

FOOD FOR THOUGHT:

Chicken cooks at about 7 minutes per pound; however, when it is in small cubes as in these appetizers the time will be shorter. Very similar to conventional cooking!

Chicken Wingettes

         12 to 16   chicken wings
                2   egg whites
                2   Tbl. water
                1   envelope chicken or pork coating mix or
                    SEASONED COATING MIX (recipe on page 74)

Disjoint chicken wings, discarding tips (you will now have 2 pieces of chicken per wing). Beat egg whites and water together. Dip each piece of chicken in egg white-water mixture; roll in coating. Place 10 to 12 pieces on a suitable serving plate or in a utility dish. The thickest portion of the chicken should be to the outer edge of the dish. Cover with paper toweling and cook about 6 minutes 30 seconds or at 7 minutes per pound. Garnish plate with fresh parsley.

Makes 24 to 32 wingettes.

Variations:

Chicken Wingettes Fiesta
Combine 1 package Taco Seasoning mix and ⅓ cup fine dry bread crumbs for coating mix.

Chicken Wingettes Italiano
Coat with a mixture of ½ cup fine dry bread crumbs, 2 Tbl. Parmesan cheese, ⅛ tsp. garlic powder, ½ tsp. Italian seasonings, salt and pepper to taste. Or use ½ to 1 cup Italian seasoned bread crumbs.

Indian Curry Chicken Wingettes
Add 1 tsp. curry powder to coating mix.

* * * * * * * * * *

FOOD FOR THOUGHT:

1½ pounds chicken wings will usually yield 8 wings or 16 wingettes.

Coconut Curry Chicken Chunks

Tender pieces of chicken coated with curry-flavored coconut.

½	pound boned, skinned chicken breasts
¼	cup vermouth
2	Tbl. butter or margarine
¼	cup prepared SEASONED COATING MIX (recipe on page 74)
¼	cup fine grated coconut (available at health food stores)
¼ to ½	tsp. curry powder

Cut chicken into bite-size chunks and marinate in vermouth briefly. In a small bowl or custard cup melt the butter or margarine (this will take about 20 seconds). In another bowl mix together well the coating mix, coconut and curry powder. Spear each chicken chunk with a toothpick, dip in melted butter or margarine, and roll in coating mix. Arrange on a plate suitable for the microwave oven and serving, placing larger chunks to the outer edge of the dish. Cook covered with wax paper 3 minutes 30 seconds to 4 minutes.

Makes about 30 appetizers.

Crab Quiche Squares

The subtle flavor of crab enhances this appetizer. A lower power setting insures even cooking.

Crust:

½	cup butter or margarine
1¼	cups flour, unsifted
¾	tsp. salt

Prepare a 7½ × 11¾-inch glass utility dish by lightly greasing the bottom and sides.

In a 1½-quart bowl that is suitable for the microwave, soften the butter or margarine (this will take about 30 seconds). Blend in the flour and salt. Press evenly into prepared dish. Microwave on full power about 4 minutes 30 seconds or until it is firm and no longer doughy. Set aside to cool. Meanwhile make filling.

Filling:

1½	cups (6 oz.) shredded Jack, Swiss or Jarlsberg cheese (Jack is my favorite)
2	Tbl. flour
6	ounces crabmeat, drained and picked over to remove any cartilage
½	cup finely chopped onion
4	eggs
¾	tsp. salt
⅛	tsp. cayenne
1	cup evaporated milk or half and half, scalded Paprika
¼	cup finely minced fresh parsley

Toss together cheese and flour. Distribute evenly over cooled, cooked crust. Top with crabmeat and onion. Beat eggs, salt and cayenne together until foamy. Gradually stir in hot milk. Pour egg mixture over cheese, crab and onion. Sprinkle evenly overall with paprika, then minced parsley; keep in mind that the quiche is to be cut into bite-size squares so get some into the corners also. Microwave on full power 4 minutes; rotate the dish. Reduce the power setting to 50% and continue to cook for 15 to 17 minutes or until filling is set. Rotate the dish after 7 minutes and cover with wax paper at that time. Cool 5 to 10 minutes. Filling will continue to firm up during this time. Cut into one-inch squares. Place each square in a paper bonbon case; arrange on a serving plate with sprigs of fresh parsley for garnish, if desired. Serve warm or at room temperature.

Makes 54 squares.

FOOD FOR THOUGHT:

It will take about 2 minutes to scald one cup of milk.

If made ahead and refrigerated, reheat 20 squares on full power, uncovered, about 1 minute 45 seconds.

These freeze well: Place squares in cases, in a suitable container, with wax paper between layers. When ready to use, transfer 20 to a plate; microwave on 50% power about 5 minutes. Increase to full power and microwave about 1 minute 45 seconds or until warm.

If cooked on full power only, it will take 11 to 14 minutes. Rotate the dish 4 times during the microwave time; cover with wax paper halfway through the cooking time.

Cocktail Meatballs Italian Style

1	pound lean ground beef
¼	cup Italian seasoned bread crumbs
¼	cup grated Parmesan cheese
1	egg, slightly beaten
2	Tbl. chopped fresh parsley
½	tsp. crumbled dried oregano
1	tsp. salt
⅛	tsp. black pepper
	Paprika

Combine all ingredients, except paprika; mix thoroughly. Form into small balls and place in a suitable baking dish (a 9-inch glass cake dish works well). Sprinkle generously with paprika. Cook covered with wax paper about 5 minutes.

Makes 55 to 60 small meatballs.

FOOD FOR THOUGHT:

Paprika is a natural browning agent and will enhance the appearance by giving the meatballs a nice color.

Meatballs Olé

      1   pound lean ground beef
      1   cup fine dry bread crumbs
      1   tsp. Kitchen Bouquet or Gravy Master, optional
      1   egg, slightly beaten
      ¼   cup half and half or evaporated milk
      1   onion, minced
      ½   can (2 oz.) diced chiles
      ¼   tsp. oregano
      1   tsp. salt
      1   can (7 oz.) salsa

Combine all ingredients, except salsa. Mix well and shape into small meatballs. Cook covered with wax paper 6 minutes. Drain off excess fat, if necessary. Pour salsa over meatballs; heat about 2 minutes 30 seconds or until hot and bubbly.

Makes about 60 small meatballs.

FOOD FOR THOUGHT:

To use as a main dish over rice, use two cans of salsa; heat about 3 minutes 30 seconds.

Serves 4 with other suitable accompaniments, such as a vegetable, a tossed green salad, and a dessert.

Oriental Meatballs

For a different flavor, these use ground pork.

2	cups soft bread crumbs (about 2½ slices)
¼	cup dry sherry
2	Tbl. soy sauce
1	large clove garlic, minced fine
¼	cup finely chopped onion
1	tsp. salt
¼	tsp. pepper
¼	cup cilantro leaves, chopped fine (optional)
½-inch	piece (approximately) fresh ginger root, grated or minced fine
1	pound lean ground pork
1	can (8 oz.) water chestnuts, drained and chopped
2	Tbl. oyster sauce mixed with 1 Tbl. soy sauce
	Paprika, optional

Blend together bread crumbs with sherry, soy sauce, garlic, onion, salt, pepper, ginger and cilantro, if using; mix well. Mix in ground pork and chopped water chestnuts. Form into 1-inch balls and place on a large plate or utensil suitable for the microwave oven that has been coated with 1 Tbl. of the oyster sauce and soy sauce mixture. Brush remaining mixture over meatballs. Sprinkle with paprika. This will give extra good color to the meatballs. Cook covered with wax paper 9 to 10 minutes. Drain off grease if necessary. Stir gently. Serve with SWEET-SOUR SAUCE or BROWN SAUCE as dips; recipes on page 25.

Makes about 5 dozen small meatballs.

If desired, serve as a main dish with rice and your choice of sauce poured overall!

Sweet-Sour Sauce

An excellent dipping sauce for Oriental meatballs, won ton, or egg rolls.

1	Tbl. cornstarch
3	Tbl. cider vinegar
½	cup orange juice, pineapple juice or marmalade
½	cup brown sugar
¼	tsp. ground ginger
1	Tbl. catsup, optional
1	Tbl. soy sauce

Combine all ingredients in a two-cup suitable utensil, blending well. Cook until mixture comes to a full boil and is thickened (this will take about 2 minutes); stir two to three times during cooking.

Makes about ⅔ cup.

* * * * * * * * * *

Brown Sauce

Use as a dipping sauce for Oriental meatballs or pour over eggs, meats or Egg Foo Young.

4	tsp. cornstarch
1	cup water
2 to 3	Tbl. soy sauce
1	tsp. instant granular chicken or beef bouillon
	dash garlic powder, optional

Combine all ingredients in a 1½ to 2-cup suitable utensil. Cook, stirring two to three times, until thick and bubbly (this will take about 3 minutes 30 seconds).

One cup chicken or beef stock may be substituted for the water and bouillon, if desired.

Makes 1⅓ cups.

Meatballs in Wine Sauce

Good as an hors d'oeuvre or served with mashed potatoes, rice or noodles as a main dish.

1	pound lean ground beef
½	cup fine dry bread crumbs
¼	cup water
1	Tbl. instant fresh minced onion
1	Tbl. fresh chopped parsley or 1½ tsp. dried
1	tsp. salt
⅛	tsp. pepper
1	egg
1	package dry brown gravy mix
¼ to ½	cup red wine
¼	cup water

Mix together beef, bread crumbs, ¼ cup water, onion, parsley, salt, pepper and egg. Form into small balls and place in a 1½-quart casserole. Sprinkle meatballs with dry gravy mix and gently stir to coat each. Cook covered with wax paper 5 minutes. Pour over the wine and water; stir gently. Cook covered with wax paper an additional 3 to 4 minutes. Stir and serve with picks to spear.

Makes 55 to 60 small meatballs.

Serves 4 as a main dish when served with rice, noodles or potatoes.

FOOD FOR THOUGHT:

If you prefer, use only water for the liquid. The amount of liquid is dependent on the desired thickness and amount of gravy.

The gravy mix gives this dish good color and flavor!

Deviled Mushrooms

A good and easy recipe!

20 to 25	bite-size fresh mushrooms
1	can (2¼ oz.) deviled ham
1	Tbl. sour cream or mayonnaise
2	Tbl. minced green pepper
1½	tsp. minced onion
2	Tbl. fine dry bread crumbs

Quickly rinse mushrooms and drain well. Remove stems and save for another use. Mix together the remaining ingredients; fill mushroom caps with ham mixture and arrange on a serving plate that is suitable for the microwave oven. Cook covered with wax paper about 2 minutes 30 seconds or until heated through.

If refrigerated, cook covered with wax paper about 3 minutes.

FOOD FOR THOUGHT:

To make your own bread crumbs place a slice of bread on a piece of paper toweling in the microwave and cook 1 minute 30 seconds to 2 minutes or until almost dry; as it cools it will continue to dry. Time will vary because of freshness and type of bread being used. When dry, crush with a rolling pin or use your blender or food processor.

Italian Stuffed Mushrooms

¾	pound bite-size fresh mushrooms
½	cup soft fresh bread crumbs
1 to 2	Tbl. fresh minced parsley
1	Tbl. Parmesan cheese
1	cup (4 oz.) grated Jack or Mozzarella cheese
1	tsp. Italian seasonings, crushed between fingers
⅛	tsp. garlic powder or 1 clove garlic, finely minced
½	tsp. salt

Wash mushrooms quickly and drain well. Remove stems and chop fine. Add to remaining ingredients. Fill mushroom caps with filling, mounding slightly; place on a 10-inch plate that can be put in the microwave oven. Cook about 2 minutes 30 seconds or until cheese starts to melt.

Makes about 38.

FOOD FOR THOUGHT:

Four ounces of cheese equal 1 cup grated cheese.

Mushroom caps make perfect holders or boats for a multitude of fillings. Cooked in the microwave they taste succulent, retain their shape, and cook rapidly.

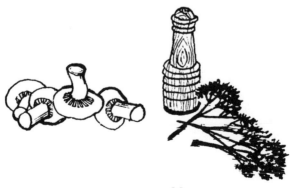

Mushrooms Florentine

Mushroom caps stuffed with a creamy spinach filling.

38 to 40   (about ¾ pound) bite-size fresh mushrooms
1   package (10 oz.) chopped frozen spinach
½   cup sour cream
½   tsp. Worcestershire sauce
3   Tbl. dry onion soup mix

Prepare mushrooms by washing quickly and draining well. Remove stems and reserve for another use. Place package of spinach in carton on a triple layer of paper toweling or in a glass utility dish in the microwave oven; cook on full power 4 to 5 minutes. Set aside until cool enough to handle. Squeeze out excess moisture from spinach; mix in sour cream, Worcestershire sauce, and dry onion soup mix. Fill prepared mushroom caps with mixture, mounding slightly. Place on a serving plate that can also be used in the microwave oven. Cook covered with wax paper 3 minutes to 3 minutes 30 seconds.

Makes 38 to 40 appetizers.

If made ahead and refrigerated, cook covered with wax paper; add one minute cooking time or heat until hot through.

FOOD FOR THOUGHT:
Use extra-large mushrooms and serve as an accompaniment to roast beef.

Mushrooms Parmesan

Easy, quick, and delicious!

          ½   pound small fresh mushrooms
          2   Tbl. butter
    1 to 2   Tbl. Parmesan cheese
               Seasoned salt or garlic salt to taste,
     OR 1   clove garlic, minced fine, and salt to taste

Wash mushrooms quickly and drain well. For best appearance cut stem flush with cap. In a shallow dish melt butter (this will take about 20 seconds). Blend in cheese and seasonings; add mushrooms, stirring to coat with seasoned butter mixture. Cook 2 minutes 30 seconds to 3 minutes or until hot.

For variety add sesame seed, chopped fresh parsley, or chives.

FOOD FOR THOUGHT:

There are about 25 small fresh mushrooms in a half pound, which should serve as an hors d'oeuvre for four.

It's the seasoning on these that makes them so good; don't skimp!

Sesame Baked Mushrooms

         1   pound fresh mushrooms (small to medium size)
        ½   cup fine dry bread crumbs, preferably Italian
                 seasoned
        ¼   cup sesame seed
½ to ¾   tsp. salt
        ⅛   tsp. pepper
        ½   tsp. paprika
         1   egg white
         1   Tbl. water

Wash mushrooms quickly and drain well. Trim stems flush with caps. Mix together with the bread crumbs, sesame seed, salt, pepper and paprika. In a bowl large enough to hold all the mushrooms beat the egg white with water. Place mushrooms in egg white mixture and gently stir to coat well. Take a few mushrooms at a time and roll in bread crumb mixture, removing with a slotted spoon to a suitable serving platter that can be used in the microwave oven. Cook uncovered 5 minutes. Garnish platter with parsley or celery leaves. Serve hot, using picks to spear the mushrooms.

Makes 50 to 60.

FOOD FOR THOUGHT:

If you don't have Italian seasoned bread crumbs, use regular bread crumbs and season with 1 Tbl. Parmesan cheese, ½ tsp. Italian seasonings, crushed, and ⅛ tsp. garlic powder.

31

Shrimp Stuffed Mushrooms

A delicate flavor combination.

35 to 40	bite-size mushrooms
1	can (2½ oz.) shrimp, drained
¾	cup soft fresh bread crumbs (about 1½ slices)
1½	tsp. instant or 1 Tbl. fresh minced onion
1 to 2	Tbl. finely minced green pepper, optional
	Salt and pepper to taste
1	Tbl. lemon juice
1	Tbl. white wine or water
	Paprika

Wash mushrooms quickly and drain well. Remove stems and save for another use. Place shrimp, bread crumbs, onion, green pepper (if using), salt, pepper, lemon juice and water or wine in a medium-size bowl. Mix well (shrimp will break up slightly). Fill each mushroom cap with mixture, mounding slightly and firming with fingers. Sprinkle lightly with paprika. Cook covered with wax paper about 2 minutes 30 seconds. If made ahead and refrigerated, cook about 3 minutes. Garnish plate with fresh parsley before serving.

Makes 35 to 40 appetizers.

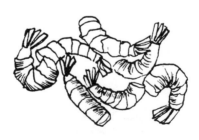

Super Stuffed Mushrooms

The flavor of these really is super!

25	small (bite-size) fresh mushrooms
¼	cup chopped almonds
1	Tbl. instant minced onion
1	Tbl. lemon juice
½	cup (about 1 slice) soft fresh bread crumbs
½	tsp. salt or to taste
⅛	tsp. garlic powder, optional
1 to 2	Tbl. sherry or water
	Paprika

Wash mushrooms quickly and drain well. Remove stems and chop fine; mix with remaining ingredients, except paprika. Fill mushroom caps with mixture, mounding slightly and firming gently with fingers. Sprinkle with paprika. Cook covered with wax paper 2 minutes 30 seconds. If prepared ahead and refrigerated, cook about 3 minutes. Garnish plate with fresh parsley before serving.

Makes 25 appetizers.

FOOD FOR THOUGHT:
One pound of mushrooms contains only 66 to 100 calories!

33

Teriyaki Beef Kabob Appetizers

¾ pound (after trimming) sirloin or top round steak,
    well trimmed of fat
1   can (20-ounce) pineapple chunks or 2½ cups fresh
    pineapple cut into small chunks
1   small green pepper, cut into small chunks
¼   cup bottled or the following teriyaki marinade

Teriyaki Marinade

¼   cup soy sauce
2   Tbl. sherry wine
3   Tbl. brown sugar
1   large clove garlic, finely minced
1   tsp. grated fresh ginger or ¾ tsp. ground ginger
2   tsp. flour

Cut steak into bite-size pieces, about the same size as the pine-apple chunks. Combine soy sauce, sherry, brown sugar, ginger, garlic and flour. Pour marinade over meat pieces; stir well to coat. Set aside at room temperature to marinate for at least one hour. Stir once or twice during this time to keep meat well coated with mixture. On a sandwich pick or bamboo skewer place a meat piece, green pepper chunk and pineapple chunk. On a utensil suitable for the microwave and one you can serve from, arrange the kabobs in a circle, spoke fashion. Cook 24 kabobs, uncovered, ap-proximately 4 minutes or until meat is just slightly pink. Cook 48 kabobs approximately 5 minutes.

Makes about 48 appetizer kabobs.

FOOD FOR THOUGHT:

If you want to make a smaller amount of kabobs, use an 8-ounce can of pineapple; it will contain about 18 pieces. Follow above cooking instructions; microwave approximately 3 minutes.

If desired, cook green pepper chunks briefly before skewering for about 1 minute.

Appetizer Beef Bites

An Oriental flavor!

2	Tbl. sesame seed
1	tsp. butter or margarine
¾	pound top round or sirloin steak
2	Tbl. soy sauce
2	Tbl. catsup
1	tsp. prepared mustard
½	tsp. paprika
½	tsp. cornstarch
1	Tbl. oil
⅛	tsp. *each* garlic powder, ginger, pepper
¼	tsp. salt
2	Tbl. minced green onion, optional

In a small dish or custard cup place the sesame seed with the butter or margarine. Cook uncovered stirring each 15 seconds, until sesame seed is lightly toasted; this will take about 2 minutes. Set aside.

Cut meat into bite-size pieces. Mix remaining ingredients and pour over meat; mix well to coat pieces with marinade. Marinate 1 to 2 hours, stirring occasionally. When meat has marinated sufficiently, cook covered with a paper towel about 3 minutes, stirring once during cooking. Sprinkle with the toasted sesame seeds and green onion. Spear with toothpicks to serve.

Makes 4 servings as an appetizer.

A similar hors d'oeuvre is TERIYAKI BEEF KABOBS; recipe is on page 34.

Tuna Nuggets

1 can (7 oz.) tuna, well drained
2 Tbl. each minced onion and fresh parsley
4 Tbl. mayonnaise
1 egg, beaten
½ cup fine dry bread crumbs
2 tsp. prepared mustard
⅛ tsp. each thyme and cayenne
⅛ tsp. sage or ¼ tsp. curry powder
　Approximately ½ cup crumb coating such as Shake 'n
　　Bake for fish, cornflake crumbs, or toasted
　　bread crumbs
　Paprika

Combine all ingredients, except crumb coating and paprika, mixing well. Roll into balls, using approximately 2 teaspoons for each. Roll in the crumb coating (my favorite is Shake 'n Bake for fish). Place on a dish suitable for the microwave oven or on a pie plate. Sprinkle with paprika and cook uncovered 5 minutes. Garnish plate with fresh parsley or celery leaves.

Makes about 24 appetizers.

Good served hot or cold, plain or with a tartar sauce dip.

Zucchini Squares

1¾ to 2   cups lightly packed shredded zucchini
2   Tbl. minced onion
2   Tbl. olive oil
¼   cup fine dry bread crumbs
1   small clove garlic, minced fine
¾   cup shredded Jack cheese
2   Tbl. minced fresh parsley
½   tsp. each salt and pepper
2   eggs, well beaten

Topping:

2   Tbl. fine dry bread crumbs
1   Tbl. Parmesan cheese
  Paprika

In a utensil suitable for the microwave oven cook the zucchini and onion in olive oil for about 2 minutes. Add remaining ingredients, except topping, mixing well. Pour into a lightly oiled 6 × 10-inch glass utility dish. Combine bread crumbs and Parmesan cheese. Distribute evenly over top of zucchini mixture. Sprinkle lightly with paprika. Cook covered with wax paper 5 to 6 minutes or until firm. Cool and cut into one-inch squares.

FOOD FOR THOUGHT:

For easier serving, place squares in paper bonbon cases before placing on serving plate.

This can also be cut into larger squares and be served as a vegetable dish at lunch or dinner.

Smoked Almonds

A delicious cocktail nut!

1	cup whole almonds with skins on
2	tsp. water
1	tsp. *each* salt, liquid smoke and salad oil
¼	tsp. browning sauce, such as Kitchen Bouquet or Gravy Master
¼	tsp. garlic powder
1	tsp. flour

Combine liquid smoke, water and ½ tsp. of the salt in a glass or ceramic 9-inch pie plate. Add almonds; mix well to coat. Cover and soak at least 2 hours; stir after 1 hour. Drizzle salad oil and browning agent over nuts; mix well to coat. Sprinkle with garlic powder, flour, and remaining ½ tsp. salt. Toss until well coated with mixture. Cook uncovered on full power 5 to 6 minutes, stirring 2 to 3 times during cooking.

Nuts should be well browned and roasted. If desired, sprinkle with additional salt while still hot. Cool and store in airtight container. These are best if made a day or two before serving.

For one pound of nuts (3 cups) triple other ingredients. Cook in a 7½ × 11¾-inch glass utility dish, uncovered, about 10 minutes, stirring every 2 to 3 minutes.

FOOD FOR THOUGHT:

Cooking times will vary with age of nuts. Watch carefully during microwave time, as they can scorch and burn easily.

These make an excellent gift at Christmas, or any time, for that matter! Put the nuts in a decorative container or just a plastic bag tied with a bow.

Bacon Crisps

My favorite easy appetizer!

    4   slices bacon, cut into fourths
    8   Triscuit crackers, broken in half

Wrap a piece of bacon around each cracker half; lay lapped side down on a paper plate that is lined with 4 layers of paper toweling. Cover with another paper towel to absorb spatters; cook 4 minutes to 4 minutes 30 seconds. Take into consideration cure of bacon and thickness. (See bacon cooking instructions, indexed.) Place on a serving dish, and serve at room temperature for best flavor.

Makes 16 bite-size appetizers.

* * * * * * * * * *

Party Mix My Way

. . . Also known as Nuts 'n Bolts

      1   cup *each* almonds, brazil nuts and cashews
    1½   cups *each* pretzels, Cheerios, Kix, and Wheat Chex
          cereals
      ½   cup margarine
      2   Tbl. Worcestershire sauce
      1   tsp. celery salt
      ½   tsp. *each* garlic and onion powders

In a 7½ × 11¾-inch glass utility dish place the nuts and cereals. In a small utensil suitable for the microwave (a glass measuring cup works well), melt the margarine together with the seasonings. Pour over the cereal nut mixture, stirring to coat well. Cook in the microwave 10 to 12 minutes, stirring every 3 minutes. Cool and store in sealed containers.

Makes about 9 cups.

Seasoned Oyster Crackers

Serve in place of nuts, with cheese, or as a garnish for soup.

¼   cup butter or margarine
½   tsp. paprika
½   tsp. salt
¼   tsp. *each* garlic powder, onion powder, thyme and sage
     Salt and pepper to taste
1   box (12 oz.) oyster crackers

In a 2-quart casserole or similar utensil melt together the butter or margarine, seasonings and salt (this will take about 30 seconds). Add the oyster crackers and stir to coat well with mixture. Cook 4 minutes, stirring after 2 minutes and at end of cooking time. Let cool before serving.

* * * * * * * * *

Chili Nuts

Good and spicy!

2   Tbl. butter or margarine
1   (12 oz.) jar dry roasted peanuts
3   Tbl. dry chili mix or Spanish rice seasoning mix

Melt butter or margarine in a shallow baking dish or pie plate; stir in peanuts, coating well with butter or margarine. Sprinkle with dry chili mix and stir again. Cook 5 minutes, stirring once or twice during cooking. Cool before serving for best flavor.

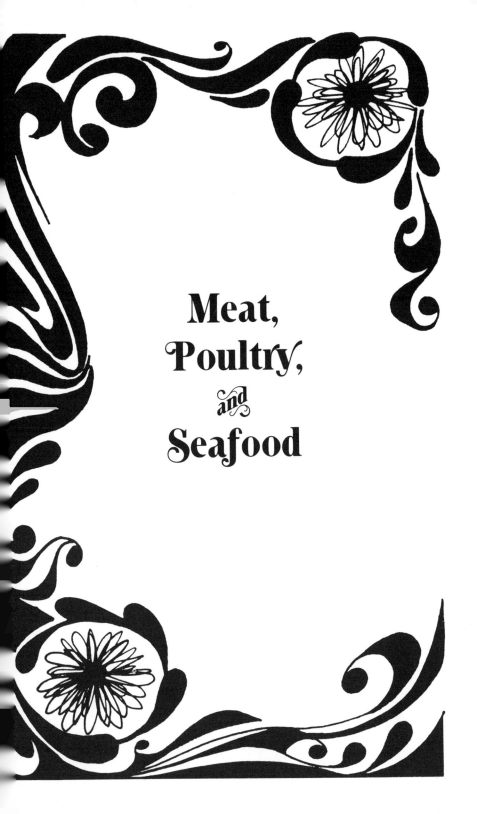

Meat, Poultry, and Seafood

MEATS

It is best to choose tender cuts of meat for roasting. However, less tender cuts can be cooked with great success if you have a microwave oven with variable power or a defrost cycle.

Factors that affect the cooking times (number of minutes per pound) are: tenderness of cut, starting temperature of meat, shape or thickness of meat, microwave power setting, and most important, personal preference as to doneness.

Check the times given in your microwave manufacturer's cookbook as a guide to follow.

A roast will cook more evenly if the length is greater than the diameter and if the meat is at room temperature before cooking. You might compare this to barbecuing. Meats that are frozen should be defrosted before cooking to insure that the center will not be frozen or cold at the end of the cooking time.

To obtain even cooking, begin roasts with the fat side down; turn over after half the cooking time. Natural browning will begin to occur with meat cooked over 10 to 12 minutes because of the fat content, heat generated and length of the cooking time involved. However, there will not be a crusty surface, because the microwave oven lacks the dry heat needed to evaporate away the surface moisture.

There are numerous off-the-shelf items that can enhance the appearance of meats. Paprika is one of my favorites and it doesn't add any flavor if used sparingly. Dry onion soup mix adds texture along with good flavor. Dry brown gravy mix gives good color and flavor too (if put in a shaker, it's convenient to use on small meats such as hamburgers). Browning sauces and other agents (see page 216) can also be used.

A standing time is necessary for roasts, just as required in conventional cooking. The internal temperature will continue to rise 15 to 20 degrees while standing after cooking, so take this into consideration when using the temperature probe, which registers the internal temperature of the food, or when testing with a meat thermometer. Quick-registering thermometers that give temperature readings almost instantly are now available. Some of these may be used in the microwave oven while cooking; follow the manufacturer's care and use instructions. It's advisable to have more food in relation to the amount of metal when cooking in the microwave. Metal utensils, foil, or thermometers should be kept at least one-inch away from the walls of the oven to prevent arcing. This arcing could damage the oven walls. Do not use a conventional thermometer in the microwave while cooking, only a special microwave thermometer.

Cover meats with paper toweling or wax paper to prevent spatters from going on the oven walls, except with pot roasts, etc., where moist heat is required. With these it will be necessary to cover with a casserole lid to retain the steam or moisture. Cooking bags may also be used. If bag has foil strip on end, cut off and discard. DO NOT use the metal twist tie to close; use a rubber band or string. If you do not seal tightly and allow some steam to escape, slits in the bag will not be necessary, thereby allowing you to turn the bag over for even cooking of the meat. Place the bag with the meat in a glass utility dish to be on the safe side, in case juices leak out.

You'll have more pan drippings for gravy when cooking in the microwave, as they do not evaporate as fast. If you draw them off during cooking (use a baster or spoon), the meat or poultry will cook slightly faster since you will be decreasing the load. The drippings can be saved for making gravy after the meat has cooked.

Meats can be reheated easily without drying out or further cooking. Take care not to reheat too long, so that they begin to cook again. Cover with wax paper or plastic wrap and microwave just until heated through. The volume, thickness, and beginning temperature will determine the amount of time involved.

Bacon

You'll find bacon tastes extra good when cooked in the microwave oven; it's so easy to cook you'll serve it often, and won't hesitate when a recipe calls for only a couple of slices for garnishing.

For easy cleanup, bacon may be cooked on paper toweling and a paper plate. I have found up to 5 slices work best. With more than that there is too much grease to be absorbed into the paper. However, if a small amount of grease does go through, just wipe it up with another paper towel. Easy!

Usually 4 sheets of paper toweling and one paper plate (for ease in getting the bacon in and out of the oven) work well; cover the strips with another paper towel to prevent spattering of the oven walls.

The suggested cooking time is approximately one minute per slice. Here again, personal preference along with thickness of bacon slices are determining factors.

Certain cures of bacon, as in the case of slab bacon and canned bacon, will vary greatly as to timing, so watch carefully while experimenting with cooking times to suit your personal preference.

You can cook up to a half pound at a time layering between paper towels in a glass utility dish, or use a special bacon rack for microwave cooking.

If you like to save bacon grease for other cooking purposes, use the bacon rack. I still like to use a paper towel between the rack and the slices; while you lose a small amount of the grease, it is also being strained, leaving almost pure white fat. Don't forget to cover with a paper towel to absorb those grease spatters!

Beef Rolls

4   cube steaks (1¾ to 2 pounds)
1   can (8 oz.) tomato sauce
2   Tbl. vinegar
3   Tbl. oil
     Salt and pepper to taste
⅛   tsp. garlic powder or 1 clove garlic, minced fine
½   tsp. oregano, crushed

Stuffing:
1½   cups dry bread stuffing mix
½   cup chopped celery
¼   cup chopped onion
2   Tbl. chopped fresh parsley
     Approximately 5 small fresh mushrooms, thinly sliced
½   tsp. salt
3   Tbl. water or white wine

Mix together tomato sauce, vinegar, oil, salt, pepper, garlic and oregano. Marinate cube steaks in mixture for approximately ½ hour. While meat is marinating, combine ingredients for stuffing. Place ½ cup of stuffing mixture down center of each steak. Roll and place seam side down in a 1½-quart baking dish that is suitable for the microwave oven. Leave space between rolls. Spoon any remaining marinade over each. (At this point the beef rolls may be refrigerated for a later cooking time.) If refrigerated, cook covered with wax paper about 15 minutes, rotating dish halfway through cooking time. If cooked immediately and at room temperature, microwave covered with wax paper about 12 minutes, rotating dish halfway through cooking time. Garnish with chopped fresh parsley if desired.

Makes 4 generous servings.

Good accompaniments are SPECIAL SPINACH, BAKED TOMATOES, for which recipes are indexed, a tossed green salad and, of course, dessert.

Bonus Burgers

Make 'burgers special by stuffing with fresh mushrooms or cheese. A real bonus!

    1½   pounds lean ground beef
    ½   pound fresh mushrooms or 4 oz. cheddar cheese, cut
            into fingers
    1   package dry brown gravy mix

Divide ground beef into 8 equal portions. Shape each portion into a patty. Top 4 of the patties with one or two sliced mushrooms, depending on size, or a cheese finger. Sprinkle with one teaspoon dry gravy mix. Top these 4 with remaining patties, pressing edges together; shape into ovals. Pour remaining dry gravy mix onto a plate and dip each stuffed burger into the mix, coating well. Place in an 8-inch-square glass baking dish or other suitable utensil. Slice remaining mushrooms and place on top of burgers. Salt and pepper lightly. Cook covered with wax paper about 7 minutes.

Makes 4 servings.

FOOD FOR THOUGHT:

One-half pound of mushrooms equals about 8 large or 25 medium.

Brown gravy mix not only gives good flavor but adds color to this quick-cooking meat dish.

Liver, Bacon and Onions Grace's Way

6	slices bacon, cut in 1-inch pieces
1½	pounds beef liver
¼	cup soy sauce
¾	cup flour
1	tsp. salt
¼	tsp. pepper
1	tsp. paprika
⅛	tsp. garlic powder
2	medium onions, sliced
	Salt to taste

In a 7½ × 11¾-inch glass utility dish place bacon. Microwave covered with paper toweling about 6 minutes or until crisp. Stir periodically to keep pieces separated. Remove with a slotted spoon and set aside. While bacon is cooking, dip liver in soy sauce and dredge in a mixture of flour, salt, pepper, paprika, and garlic powder. Place coated liver into hot bacon fat. Top with sliced onions; salt to taste. Cook covered with wax paper about 10 minutes. Top with cooked bacon and serve.

Makes 4 to 5 servings.

FOOD FOR THOUGHT:

If you feel too much bacon fat has accumulated, drain some of it off.

Indexed under Appetizers, see:

MEATBALLS IN WINE SAUCE, on page 26, and

ORIENTAL MEATBALLS, page 24.

Both make excellent main dishes.

Meatloaf au Gratin

A nice change from the typical meatloaf. My students say it's a winner.

½	cup chopped onion
¼	cup chopped green pepper
1	can (8 oz.) tomato sauce; reserve 2 oz. for topping
1	egg
½	cup quick-cooking oats
½	tsp. salt or to taste
⅛	tsp. garlic powder or 1 clove garlic, minced
⅛	tsp. pepper
1	tsp. instant granular chicken bouillon
¼	tsp. thyme
1¾	pounds lean ground beef
1	cup (4 oz.) ½-inch cubes sharp cheddar cheese
1	Tbl. dry bread crumbs, optional
	Paprika

In a large mixing bowl blend together the onion, green pepper, 6 ounces of the tomato sauce, egg, oatmeal and seasonings. Mix in ground beef and add cheese cubes, distributing as evenly as possible. Place meat mixture in a suitable baking dish; for quick even cooking shape meat mixture like a large doughnut. In the center place a small heavy duty glass or custard cup, if desired. Spoon remaining tomato sauce on top of meatloaf and sprinkle with bread crumbs, paprika, and additional salt and pepper. Cook covered with wax paper 15 to 17 minutes. If using a temperature sensor, set temperature to 150 degrees. Draw off juices during cooking once or twice if necessary. Let stand 5 to 10 minutes for easier slicing.

Makes 6 to 8 servings.

FOOD FOR THOUGHT:

When molding meatloaf, surround cheese cubes completely with meat mixture to keep melting cheese from running out.

Souper Easy Meatloaf

¼ cup chili sauce, catsup or tomato sauce
1   package dry onion soup mix
⅓ cup quick-cooking oats
1   egg
1   tsp. Worcestershire sauce
1   tsp. salt
⅛ tsp. garlic powder or 1 clove finely minced garlic
1½ pounds lean ground beef
    Salt, pepper, and paprika

Combine chili sauce, catsup or tomato sauce with the dry onion soup mix, oatmeal, egg, Worcestershire sauce, salt and garlic powder. Add ground beef; mix well. Place in a suitable baking dish and shape into a ring (like a doughnut). If desired, place a custard cup or small heavy-duty glass in the center to help meat retain its shape while cooking. Season top with salt and pepper; sprinkle generously with paprika. Cook covered with wax paper 10 to 12 minutes. If using a temperature sensor, set temperature to 150 degrees. Cook on full power. Let rest at least 5 minutes before slicing.

Makes 5 to 6 servings.

FOOD FOR THOUGHT:

Paprika is a natural browning agent; it gives the meat good color and enhances the appearance.

Tasty Pork Chops

4 pork chops about ½-inch thick
1 package dry onion soup mix
½ tsp. garlic salt, optional

Pour dry onion soup mix in a dish or on a paper plate. Dip pork chops into dry mixture, coating each side well. Place the coated chops into an 8-inch-square glass utility dish or other suitable baking dish with meatiest portions to the outer edge of dish. Sprinkle lightly with garlic salt if using. Cook covered with wax paper about 10 minutes on full power.

FOOD FOR THOUGHT:

Pork cooks at about 9 minutes per pound on full power. If your unit has variable power, reduce power setting and extend cooking time, making the meat more tender. On 70% or ⅔ power allow about 12 minutes per pound. Pork is done when internal temperature reaches 170 to 175 degrees on meat thermometer. Cook only to 165 degrees, as the temperature will rise as it stands. Chops should be fork-tender and meat white when slashed. Be careful not to overcook or it will be dry.

Dry onion soup mix and brown gravy mix not only give good flavor, but also good color to meats that cook in a relatively short time. Because of the short cooking time meats will not brown naturally, so you must help give them eye appeal.

Pork Chops and Dressing

          4   cups (6½ oz. package) poultry dressing mix
          ¼   cup melted butter or margarine
          ¼   cup diced celery
     2 to 3   Tbl. minced onion
          1   egg, beaten
          1   cup chicken broth or ½ cup each broth and
               white wine
          4   pork chops about ½-inch thick
               Salt and pepper to taste
          1   egg white beaten with 1 Tbl. water
               Paprika

Using 3 cups of the dry dressing mix, prepare by mixing together with the melted butter or margarine, celery, onion, beaten egg and broth or combination of broth and wine. Place in a 9-inch-square utility dish or other utensil suitable for the microwave oven. Crush the remaining 1 cup dressing mix; dip chops in egg white-water mixture, then crushed dressing. Place on top of prepared dressing with larger portion of meat to outer edge of dish. Sprinkle with salt, pepper and paprika. Cook covered with plastic wrap about 12 minutes on full power or 18 to 20 minutes on 50% power. (On many microwave ovens this is the defrost cycle or medium power level.) Let rest a few minutes before serving.

Makes 3 to 4 servings.

Spicy Sausage Ring

Tasty with scrambled eggs for breakfast.

1	egg
¼	cup milk
½	cup quick-cooking oats
2	Tbl. minced onion
½	tsp. salt
¼	tsp. cumin
¼	tsp. sage
1	pound pork sausage (hot style preferred)
¾	tsp. paprika

Combine egg, milk, oats and seasonings, except paprika. Add sausage and mix well. Sprinkle paprika evenly over the bottom of a ceramic or plastic ring mold that is especially made for microwave use. If you do not have a ring mold, use a 1-quart casserole dish with a custard cup or small heavy duty glass in the center. Spoon mixture into dish and pack uniformly. Cover with wax paper and cook 11 to 13 minutes. Drain off fat. Let stand 5 to 10 minutes longer, drain off fat again if necessary. Invert onto serving platter and fill center with scrambled eggs if desired. Garnish with sprigs of fresh parsley or cilantro.

Makes 4 or 5 servings.

FOOD FOR THOUGHT:

A recipe and a half cooks in 13 to 15 minutes.

A double recipe will cook in 16 to 18 minutes.

The paprika gives this sausage ring especially good color!

POULTRY

Chicken and turkey stay moist and exceptionally juicy when cooked in the microwave; they quickly become favorites.

Pieces or whole birds cook satisfactorily. With large amounts you'll find some browning occurs because of the fat content beneath the skin, the heat generated, and the length of time involved. I like to sprinkle the poultry generously with paprika for good color and eye appeal. However, browning sauces or a soy-butter or oil combination rubbed on the skin also works well. Experiment to see what suits you best! I also salt and season lightly. This is a personal preference and one you should decide in order to obtain the end result you like best.

Poultry should be defrosted and patted dry with paper toweling before cooking; this helps reduce excess moisture.

Arrange chicken pieces so that the meatiest portion is to the outer edge of the utensil, rearranging pieces once or twice during cooking if you're cooking 2 to 3 pounds at a time.

Cover with paper toweling or wax paper to prevent spatters in the oven.

When cooking poultry whole, I have found that trussing the bird (tying the wings and legs close to the body) will make it a more even shape, easier to handle, and it will cook more evenly.

Chicken cooks at approximately 7 minutes per pound on full power and at about 10 minutes per pound on 70% power (on some microwaves this is the bake or medium high setting).

Turkey cooks at about 8 minutes per pound on full power or at about 10 minutes per pound on a bake or roast setting. For best results, cook up to a 14-pound turkey in the microwave. Larger turkeys will require less attention when cooked conventionally.

For full power cooking divide the microwave time in fourths. Start cooking with the breast side down, after one-fourth of the cooking time turn to a wing side down. Repeat after an additional one-fourth cooking time for the other side. For remaining quarter cook with breast side up. Baste with pan drippings after each turn.

When you lower the power setting, because of slower cooking it is possible you will need to turn the bird over only at the halfway point.

If you find that thin portions, such as wings, are overcooking, you may shield with a thin piece of foil (refer to your owner's manual).

As excess drippings accumulate in the bottom of the dish, remove by drawing off with a baster or spoon. By doing so, moisture is reduced, therefore so is the cooking time. Save the drippings for gravy, which you can make in the microwave during the rest period after cooking your poultry. As in conventional cooking, poultry should rest before cutting to allow the juices to set and for easier carving.

MORE FOOD FOR THOUGHT:

Cook chicken parts quickly for salads, sandwiches, etc. One breast will cook covered in about 4 minutes.

Try speeding up your barbecue procedure by precooking chicken partially in the microwave and finishing up on the grill.

Leftover barbecued chicken reheats nicely in the microwave!

Chile Chicken

Chicken with a Mexican flair!

6 to 8	pieces chicken (about 2 pounds)
1	package dry chili seasoning mix
1	tsp. salt
½	cup fine dry bread crumbs
1	can (16 oz.) tomatoes, sliced
1	small onion, slivered
1	small can (4 oz.) green chiles, cut in short strips
½	cup dry white wine

Combine seasoning mix, salt and bread crumbs. Roll chicken pieces in mixture. Arrange in a casserole or glass utility dish with meatiest portions to the outer edge. Cover with paper toweling and cook 7 minutes. Arrange over top of chicken the sliced onion, chiles and tomato slices with their liquid, and wine. Cover with plastic wrap or casserole lid; cook about 9 minutes or until chicken is tender. If desired remove chicken to a platter and thicken sauce by mixing 2 Tbl. flour with 2 Tbl. water; stir into pan juices. Cook 3 minutes, stirring once or twice during cooking; pour over chicken or serve separately.

Makes 3 to 4 servings.

Good served with plain hot cooked rice, or SOUR CREAM HERBED POTATOES (recipe on page 96), a tossed green salad, and for dessert, STRAWBERRIES 'N' CREAM CAKE; recipe is on page 165.

Crab Stuffed Chicken Breasts

An elegant but easy entree with a superb flavor.
This dish is pictured on the cover.

4 chicken breasts, halved, skinned and boned
(about 1½ pounds meat)
2 Tbl. each finely chopped green onion, green
pepper and fresh parsley
6 ounces crabmeat, flaked
Brandy or dry vermouth, optional
2 to 3 Tbl. melted butter
⅓ to ½ cup fine dry bread crumbs
Salt and pepper to taste
Paprika

Sauce:

½ cup sour cream
½ cup mayonnaise
1 tsp. Dijon or prepared mustard

Pound chicken breasts between plastic wrap (to prevent tearing of meat) to flatten them.

Combine sour cream, mayonnaise, and mustard in a bowl suitable for the microwave; set aside.

Mix together the onion, green pepper, parsley, crab meat, salt and pepper to taste and 2 Tbl. of the sauce. Divide mixture among the chicken cutlets; roll up, tucking in sides. In a utensil suitable for the microwave, and one you can take to the table, arrange the chicken rolls in a circle with the seam side down.

Melt the butter in a small utensil (this will take about 20 seconds). Stir in brandy or vermouth, if using; spoon evenly over chicken. Distribute bread crumbs evenly over each. Sprinkle with salt, pepper and paprika. Cover with wax paper and cook on full power 8 to 10 minutes or until chicken is no longer pink when slashed.

Heat sauce on 50% power 3 to 4 minutes or until hot, stirring two to three times. Or you may microwave on full power 1 minute 30 seconds to 2 minutes, stirring frequently. Pass sauce for individual service.

Makes 8 servings of one roll each.

FOOD FOR THOUGHT:

To make your own bread crumbs, break up 2 slices of fresh bread and process in your food processor or blender until fine. Place crumbs on a paper plate and microwave on full power 4 to 5 minutes or until dry. Stir 2 to 3 times, and watch carefully so they do not burn.

These bread crumbs will not be quite as fine as purchased ones, but give good texture to the chicken.

OK - needs more flavor

Chicken Bundles Italiano

¼ cup butter
1   tsp. Italian seasonings *(not the ones for bread)*
½ tsp. salt
⅛ tsp. pepper
¼ tsp. garlic powder or 2 small cloves garlic, minced fine
1   Tbl. fresh chopped parsley
4   ounces (approximately) Jack or Mozzarella cheese
3   whole chicken breasts, split and boned

* * * * * * * * * *

1   egg
¼ tsp. salt
1   Tbl. water
1   Tbl. olive oil
⅛ tsp. garlic powder or 1 small clove garlic, minced fine
1   cup fine dry bread crumbs (more if necessary)
⅓ cup dry white wine such as Chablis, sauterne or
      vermouth
Chopped fresh parsley for garnish, optional

In a small suitable utensil place the butter, Italian seasonings, salt, pepper, garlic and chopped parsley. Microwave about 30 seconds; stir to blend. Cut cheese into 6 equal cubes. Set aside. Pound chicken with mallet or ice cream scoop to flatten into cutlets. (Pound between sheets of plastic wrap or wax paper to prevent tearing of meat.) Spread about 1 tsp. herb-butter mixture on each cutlet. Place a cube of cheese on each and roll up, tucking in ends when possible to make a neat bundle.

In a small bowl beat together egg, salt, water, oil and garlic. Carefully dip chicken bundles in egg mixture and roll in bread crumbs, coating well. Place in a suitable utensil or on a platter with smaller bundles to center of dish. Sprinkle generously with paprika and lightly with additional salt and pepper. (May be refrigerated at this point for later cooking. Allow 1 to 2 minutes additional microwave time.) If to be cooked at once, cover with wax paper and cook on full power about 8 minutes. Rotate the dish once or twice if necessary to insure even cooking. Meanwhile mix remaining egg mixture with any remaining herb-butter mixture and wine. Pour around cooked chicken and microwave an additional 4 to 5 minutes or until chicken is tender. If desired, garnish with chopped parsley. Let stand 2 to 3 minutes before serving. As each portion is served, see that some of the sauce is served with it.

Makes 6 servings, allowing one bundle per serving.

I suggest serving on a bed of hot PARSLIED RICE, recipe on page 104, with a vegetable such as fresh zucchini, a tossed green salad with oil and vinegar dressing, and a light fruit dessert. You might try the SPICED FRUIT COMPOTE, for which the recipe is on page 175.

FOOD FOR THOUGHT:

Chilling the chicken bundles before dipping them in the egg mixture and rolling in crumbs makes handling easier!

Curried Chicken with Hot Sherried Peaches

1   can (16 oz.) peach halves
3   Tbl. sherry
       Chicken breasts or other pieces (about 8)
¼   cup sherry or vermouth
       Prepared chicken coating mix (Shake 'n Bake or see
          recipe for SEASONED COATING MIX on page 74)
1   tsp. curry powder
1   Tbl. butter
⅓   cup brown sugar or to taste

Drain peach halves well and marinate in 3 Tbl. sherry; set aside. Dip chicken pieces in the ¼ cup wine and roll in coating mix in which the curry powder has been mixed. Place on a large platter that is suitable for the microwave oven, preferably one which you can take to the table for service. Place the thickest portions of the chicken pieces to the outer edge of dish. Cover with paper toweling and cook at approximately 7 minutes per pound on full power. Remove from oven and place peach halves around chicken; dot with butter and sprinkle with brown sugar. Return to oven and cook uncovered until hot, about 3 minutes. Garnish with parsley or celery leaves.

Makes about 4 servings.

Chicken Parmesan

A good company dish.

2	whole chicken breasts
½	cup fine dry bread crumbs
¼	cup grated Parmesan cheese
1	egg
½	tsp. salt
¼	tsp. pepper
⅛	tsp. garlic powder or 1 clove garlic, finely minced
1	can (8 oz.) tomato sauce
	Crushed oregano, salt and pepper to taste
1	cup shredded Mozzarella cheese
¼	cup grated Parmesan cheese

Cut chicken breasts in half, bone and skin. Mix together with bread crumbs and ¼ cup Parmesan cheese. Beat egg with ½ tsp. salt, ¼ tsp. pepper, and garlic. Dip each chicken breast half in egg mixture, then in the crumb mixture. Tuck ends under to form a bundle and place on a suitable baking dish or platter.* Cook covered for 7 minutes per pound. Top each portion with tomato sauce. Sprinkle generously with crushed oregano, salt and pepper. Cook an additional 2 minutes. Top with shredded Mozzarella and grated Parmesan cheese.

Makes 4 servings.

FOOD FOR THOUGHT:

*Chicken may be refrigerated at this point for cooking at a later time. Allow 1 to 2 minutes additional microwave time.

1½ pounds chicken breasts after they are skinned and boned usually yield about 1 pound of meat.

Poultry is done when juices run clear and meat is no longer pink when slashed.

Sesame Chicken with Dressing

4	cups (6½-oz. package) herb dressing mix
¼	cup diced celery
2	Tbl. minced onion
1¼	cup chicken broth or ¾ cup broth and ½ cup dry white wine
2	Tbl. sesame seed
3	large chicken breasts, split and boned if desired
¼	cup melted butter or margarine
	Salt to taste
	Paprika and fresh parsley for garnish

Toss together 3 cups of the dressing mix with the celery, onion, and liquid. Put into a suitable utensil. Crush the remaining 1 cup of dressing and add sesame seed; mix well. In a small dish melt margarine or butter (this will take about 30 seconds). Dip chicken pieces in melted butter or margarine and roll in crushed dressing mixture. Place on top of prepared dressing. Sprinkle each piece with paprika and salt to taste. Cover with wax paper and cook about 14 minutes. Rotate dish halfway through cooking time. Garnish with parsley, if desired.

Makes 4 to 6 servings.

FOOD FOR THOUGHT:

For broth, use 1 cube or 1 tsp. instant granular bouillon for each cup of liquid.

Chicken cooks at about 7 minutes per pound.

For even cooking tuck thinner portions of boned chicken under, forming a bundle of uniform thickness, or place meatier portions to the outside edge of the dish.

Oriental Turkey Patties

The use of ground turkey meat gives a nice change in flavor. It's also lower in calories than beef!

1	pound ground turkey meat (raw)
¼	cup dry fine bread crumbs
1	egg, beaten
1	Tbl. dry sherry, optional
2	tsp. brown sugar
1	tsp. ground ginger
1	clove garlic, finely minced
¼	cup finely minced onion
½	tsp. salt

* * * * * * * * * *

4	tsp. soy sauce
	Freshly ground black pepper
	Sesame seed, optional
	Paprika

Mix together the turkey, bread crumbs, egg, sherry, brown sugar, ginger, garlic, onion and salt. Divide mixture into 4 equal portions and shape into oval patties. Place in a 6 × 10-inch glass utility dish or other suitable utensil. Make 2 or 3 shallow indentations on top and spoon 1 tsp. soy sauce over each patty. Sprinkle with fresh ground pepper, sesame seed and paprika. Cook covered with wax paper about 6 minutes.

Makes 4 servings.

For variation serve with SWEET-SOUR SAUCE; recipe is on page 198.

Rice and green peas make good accompaniments!

FOOD FOR THOUGHT:

Ground turkey meat is now readily available both fresh at the meat counter and in frozen one-pound rolls in the freezer section at your grocery store.

Pojarski Cutlets

A recipe with a Polish influence!

	1	pound ground turkey meat or veal (raw)
	1	cup soft fresh bread crumbs
	¼	cup cream
	1	tsp. salt or to taste
About	½	tsp. fresh ground black pepper
	1	egg, slightly beaten
	1	package coating mix for pork or chicken or see SEASONED COATING MIX, page 74
		Paprika
	½	pound fresh mushrooms, sliced
		Salt and pepper to taste
	⅛	tsp. garlic powder or small clove garlic, minced fine
		Chopped fresh parsley for garnish

Mix together the turkey or veal, bread crumbs, cream, salt, pepper and egg. Form into four to six cakes, shaping into rounds, ovals, or cutlets. Dip both sides into coating mix. Place in a glass utility dish or on a large pie plate. Sprinkle liberally with paprika. Cook covered with wax paper 7 minutes 30 seconds to 8 minutes. Remove to a warm platter and arrange cutlets overlapping. In the same utensil the cutlets were cooked in place the sliced mushrooms; sprinkle with salt, pepper and garlic. Cook covered with wax paper about 2 minutes. Arrange around cutlets on platter. Garnish cutlets generously with chopped fresh parsley before serving.

FOOD FOR THOUGHT:

Ground turkey meat is readily available and is more economical than veal. It's also low in calories!

Rabbit Dijon

An intriguing flavor!

1	2-pound rabbit, cut up
½	cup dry white wine
⅛	tsp. garlic powder or 1 small clove garlic, minced fine
1½	tsp. salt
2	Tbl. butter or margarine
1	Tbl. Dijon mustard
¼	cup fine dry bread crumbs
	Paprika, pepper to taste and chopped fresh parsley

Marinate rabbit in wine, garlic and 1 tsp. salt for 15 to 30 minutes. In a small bowl suitable for the microwave oven, melt the butter or margarine (this will take about 25 seconds). Stir in mustard, ½ tsp. salt and 2 Tbl. of the bread crumbs. Sprinkle 1 Tbl. of the crumbs over the bottom of the cooking platter or utensil. Drain rabbit; spread mustard mixture over pieces and place on prepared utensil with the meatiest portions to the outside edge of the dish. Sprinkle pieces with remaining bread crumbs, paprika and pepper. Cook covered with wax paper about 13 minutes 30 seconds or until tender. Rotate dish once or twice during cooking to insure even cooking. Let stand 3 to 5 minutes before serving, to let juices set and for best flavor. Garnish generously with chopped fresh parsley.

Makes 3 to 4 servings.

FOOD FOR THOUGHT:

The bread crumbs and pan juices blend together to form a thin gravy which can be served with the rabbit if desired.

If you don't care for rabbit, substitute chicken! Cook at 7 minutes per pound.

SEAFOOD

Seafood cooks very rapidly and remains moist if not overcooked. As in conventional cooking, the flavor and appearance of seafood are enhanced if brushed with melted butter and sprinkled with paprika before cooking. Test for doneness with a fork. Fish should flake easily when done.

Cook on full power at 5 to 6 minutes per pound. Logically, thinner fillets will cook in less time than a thicker fish.

Fish is usually cooked covered with wax paper, except when it has a crumb coating. Remember, however, that because of the lack of dry heat in the microwave oven a crisp texture will not be obtained. Also, if adding other ingredients, such as sauces, onions or rice, additional cooking time will be required.

Abalone

1   abalone, sliced and pounded

Season each abalone steak with white pepper, salt, garlic and onion powder.Top with thin slices of lemon. Cook 3 minutes. If abalone steaks have been refrigerated, cook an additional 30 to 45 seconds. Be careful not to overcook!

This is also good cut into small pieces and served as an appetizer. Spear with toothpicks to serve.

For variation, dip steaks in seasoned bread or cracker crumbs, sprinkle with paprika and cook about 2 minutes 45 seconds.

Cottage Clambake

Creamy and subtle in flavor.

1½ cups cooked rice (directions follow)
2   Tbl. *each* butter and flour
½   tsp. *each* salt and Worcestershire sauce
⅛   tsp. garlic powder or 1 small clove garlic, minced fine
⅛   tsp. cayenne or dash Tabasco
2   Tbl. finely minced onion
1   tsp. lemon juice
1   cup milk
2   cans (6½ oz. each) minced clams, well drained
1   cup cottage cheese
2   Tbl. chopped fresh parsley
4   rounded teaspoons fine dry bread crumbs
    Paprika
4   stuffed green olives, sliced

To cook rice:

In a 1-quart casserole combine ½ cup raw long grain rice and 1 cup water with 1 tsp. salt. Cook covered 11 minutes or until most of the water has been absorbed. Set aside for rice to fully absorb water while making sauce.

* * * * * * * * * *

In a 1-quart utensil melt butter (this will take about 20 seconds). Blend in flour, salt, Worcestershire sauce, garlic, cayenne, onion, lemon juice and milk. Mix well. Cook 3 minutes or until thickened, stirring 2 to 3 times during cooking. Mix in clams, cottage cheese and parsley. Fold in rice. Divide mixture among 4 individual casseroles or clam baking shells. Sprinkle each with a rounded teaspoon of bread crumbs and dust lightly with paprika. Garnish with stuffed olive slices. Heat 5 minutes 30 seconds or until hot and bubbly.

Makes 4 generous servings.

If desired, place in a 1½-quart casserole and heat 6 minutes 30 seconds or until hot and bubbly.

Fish Fillets Amandine

1	pound fresh or frozen fish fillets
2 to 3	Tbl. lemon juice
2 to 3	Tbl. melted butter
	Seasoned salt to taste
	Paprika
3 to 4	Tbl. toasted almonds

If fish is frozen, thaw by placing package on paper toweling in the microwave oven. On defrost cycle microwave 5 to 6 minutes (turning package over once). If you do not have a defrost cycle, microwave on full power approximately 3 minutes, turning package over each minute. Be cautious, as fish can easily start to cook. Defrost just enough to easily separate fish fillets.

Pat fillets dry with paper toweling. Place on a suitable serving platter and drizzle with lemon juice, then melted butter. Sprinkle with seasoned salt and paprika. Cook covered with wax paper about 5 minutes or until fish flakes easily with a fork. Garnish with toasted almonds.

To Toast Almonds:

Spread ¼ cup sliced almonds on a paper plate or other suitable utensil. Microwave on full power 4 to 6 minutes or until they are as brown as you desire. Stir occasionally during the microwave time. Or you can roast them in 1 Tbl. butter or margarine in a small custard cup for 2 minutes 30 seconds or to desired degree, stirring two to three times.

69

Seafood Supreme

A flavorful combination of fish and shrimp.

3 Tbl. butter or margarine (I use butter as it gives best flavor)
1 small green pepper, cut lengthwise in ½-inch slices (you should have ¾ to 1 cup)
¾ pound firm fish fillets, cut crosswise in 1-inch slices (I prefer greyfish or sea bass)
4 oz. or approximately 8 medium-size fresh mushrooms, sliced
1 8-oz. package peeled, deveined shrimp
Peel of ½ lemon, finely shredded
Salt and pepper to taste
1 Tbl. chopped fresh parsley and/or chopped green onion

In a 9 to 10-inch suitable utensil (a large serving platter can be used), cook green pepper slices in butter about 2 minutes 30 seconds or until just crisp tender. Stir once during cooking. Meanwhile pat fish fillets dry with paper toweling. (This is important or there will be an excess of liquid at the end of cooking.) Stir mushrooms, lemon peel, salt and pepper in with green peppers. Push aside and place fish slices and shrimp in dish. Spoon vegetable mixture over seafood. Cook covered with wax paper 6 to 7 minutes. Fish should flake easily with a fork and shrimp should be opaque when done. Stir halfway through cooking time. Garnish with chopped parsley and/or chopped green onions.

Makes 4 servings.

I like to serve this with the SIMPLE RICE CASSEROLE (recipe is on page 105), hot French bread or rolls, and a tossed green salad.

Fish Fillets with Cheese and Green Onions

Exceptionally good—I'm sure you'll like it!

1	pound fresh or frozen fish fillets
2 to 3	Tbl. lemon juice
2 to 3	Tbl. melted butter or margarine, optional
	Salt and pepper to taste
1	cup shredded cheddar cheese
2 to 3	green onions, thinly sliced

If fish is frozen, thaw by placing package on paper toweling in the microwave oven. On defrost cycle microwave 5 to 6 minutes (turning package over once). If you do not have a defrost cycle, microwave on full power approximately 3 minutes, turning package over each minute. Be cautious, as fish can easily start to cook. Defrost just enough to easily separate fish fillets.

Pat fillets dry with paper toweling. Place on a suitable serving platter and drizzle with lemon juice, then melted butter or margarine if using. Season to taste. Cook covered with wax paper about 5 minutes or until fish flakes easily with a fork. Sprinkle with cheese and green onions. Let sit for a few minutes for cheese to melt, or return to oven for 30 to 45 seconds.

Makes 3 to 4 servings.

Spanish Baked Fish Fillets

A colorful and savory way to serve fish.

1	Tbl. olive oil
1	pound fish fillets (haddock, red snapper, or greyfish)
2	Tbl. lemon juice
1	large clove garlic, finely minced
	Salt and pepper to taste
½ to 1	small onion, thinly sliced
1	large tomato, thinly sliced
1	Tbl. chopped fresh parsley

Grease a platter suitable for the microwave oven with 1 tsp. of the olive oil. Place fish fillets on the platter and drizzle with 1 Tbl. of the lemon juice; rub in the garlic, salt and pepper. Cover fish with the onion, then the tomato and chopped parsley. Drizzle with the remaining oil and lemon juice; salt and pepper to taste. Cover loosely with plastic wrap; let stand at room temperature 15 minutes for flavors to mingle. Cook on full power 5 to 6 minutes or until fish flakes easily with a fork.

Makes 3 to 4 servings.

FOOD FOR THOUGHT:

Fish cooks on full power in 5 to 6 minutes per pound, depending on thickness of fillets and beginning temperature.

San Diego Sole

A delicate seafood combination.

    4   fillets of sole or other fish (1 to 1½ pounds)
    2   Tbl. butter
    ½   pound small cooked shrimp
    ⅛   tsp. pepper
    1   can condensed cream of mushroom soup, undiluted
    ¼   cup dry sherry
          Juice of ½ lemon
    ¼   cup grated Parmesan cheese
          Paprika

Pat fillets dry with a paper towel. Place 1 tsp. butter on each fillet along with ¼ cup shrimp; sprinkle with pepper and roll up. (If fillets are small, place shrimp between two fillets and lay flat.) Place rolls seam side down in large clam baking shells or in a suitable baking dish. Blend soup, wine and lemon juice. Spoon mixture over fish rolls (about 3 Tbl. over each). Sprinkle with Parmesan cheese and paprika. Cook 7 to 8 minutes on full power or until fish flakes easily with a fork.

Makes 4 servings.

Seasoned Coating Mix

A good substitute for the popular packaged kind and a lot less expensive! Use on chicken, pork or fish.

¼	cup flour
½	cup fine dry bread crumbs or cornflake crumbs
1	tsp. instant granular chicken bouillon
½	tsp. salt
½	tsp. celery salt
⅛	tsp. each garlic powder and pepper
¼	tsp. each onion powder, ground sage and thyme
1	tsp. paprika
2	tsp. oil

Blend together all dry ingredients; add oil and mix until well dispersed throughout the mixture. Use coating for chicken pieces, pork chops or fish. Dip the item in the white of an egg and 1 Tbl. of water, which has been lightly beaten, before rolling in the coating mix, if desired.

Store unused portion in a covered container in the refrigerator if storing for a long period of time.

Makes 1 cup.

For variation:

Add to dry mixture:

½ tsp. curry powder

OR

2 Tbl. sesame seed

OR

½ tsp. each sweet basil and oregano leaves, crushed

OR

for coating fish, a little grated fresh or dried lemon peel.

Vegetables

VEGETABLES

Vegetables are especially good when cooked in the microwave oven. They remain colorful and their texture and flavor are superb. Vitamin retention is much greater also. Shorter cooking times plus the need for so little additional moisture results in less nutrients being drained away in excess cooking liquid. One of the other nice features of the microwave is that vegetables may be cooked in the same utensil they are to be served in.

Cook vegetables covered, using only the water that clings to them in washing, or their own natural moisture. However, with dense vegetables, such as green beans or carrots, for best results it's advisable to add a little water when cooking them (about 1 to 2 tablespoons per pound). I have also found it best to cook dense vegetables on full power for 2 to 3 minutes (to get the water and vegetable hot), then reduce the power to 50% and continue cooking until tender.

Most fresh vegetables cook in 6 to 7 minutes per pound on full power, double the time on 50% power. Refer to your microwave manufacturer's cookbook for a Vegetable Cooking Chart. Keep in mind that if you do not use the quantity of water stated in the chart, adjust for a lesser cooking time. Also, take into consideration personal preference as to doneness. Test in the same manner as in conventional cooking; most taste best when cooked until only crisp tender.

I like to stir in a small amount of salt before cooking vegetables, as I feel salt brings out the flavor. If you use salt, make sure the vegetable is in a steamed situation so that the salt will be dissolved during the cooking process and will not cause surface dehydration. Try cooking vegetables with and without salt and then let the decision be yours.

Each vegetable varies in size and tenderness due to age, freshness, variety, and of course, temperature. Because of this, cooking time can vary. As in conventional cooking it may be necessary to increase or decrease cooking times. It is always best to undercook, test, and cook for a longer period of time if necessary. Overcooking causes dehydration and an unsatisfactory end result.

When cooking whole vegetables such as potatoes, acorn squash, or yams, pierce and leave at least a one-inch space between them.

Frozen vegetables may be cooked in the paper or plastic containers they are purchased in, as long as the container has a slit or opening. I usually place the container on a paper towel to absorb condensation or possibly a little wax that may melt from the carton. You may, of course, cook the vegetable in a dish suitable for the microwave; place icy side up and cook covered. Halfway through the cooking time break up and stir.

Canned vegetables need only to be heated and will take approximately 2 minutes per cup.

Spanish Beans

2   slices bacon, diced
1   small onion, chopped
1   small green pepper, diced
1   clove garlic, minced fine
2   tsp. cumin
¼   tsp. cinnamon
2   cans (16 oz. each) pink or pinto beans, drained
        OR 1 cup dried pinto beans cooked (see below)
1   can (8 oz.) tomato sauce
    Salt and pepper to taste

In a 1-quart casserole cook bacon covered for 2 minutes 15 seconds. Add onion, green pepper, garlic, cumin and cinnamon. Cook covered an additional 3 minutes. Add remaining ingredients, stirring well. Heat 4 to 5 minutes or until hot through.

Makes 4 to 5 servings.

* * * * * * * * * *

To cook dried beans:

Rinse 1 cup pinto beans with cold water. Place in a 2-quart casserole with 3 cups cold water; soak overnight.

Add 1 Tbl. salt and cook covered on full power about 35 minutes or until beans are tender. If necessary, add a small amount of water during the last 15 minutes of cooking. Stir beans every 15 minutes during cooking. Proceed as above for remainder of recipe.

Creamy Cabbage

¼	cup butter or margarine, melted
½	small cabbage, shredded or chopped fine
½	medium onion, slivered
¼	tsp. salt
¼	tsp. seasoned salt
¼ to ½	tsp. caraway seed or dill weed
¼	cup sour cream or half and half

In a 1½-quart suitable casserole melt butter or margarine (it will take about 30 seconds). Mix in remaining ingredients, except sour cream or half and half. Cook covered 4 minutes. Stir in sour cream or half and half; heat about 1 minute or until hot through. Do not overheat or sour cream may separate.

Makes 3 to 4 servings.

Celestial Carrots

If you think you don't like cooked carrots, try these.

For each medium-sized carrot use:
- 1 Tbl. butter
- 1 Tbl. brown sugar
- 2 Tbl. chopped dates
- Dash salt

Shred number of carrots desired. Melt butter in a suitable casserole dish and add carrots and remaining ingredients; mix well. Cook covered. Three carrots will cook in approximately 4 minutes; for each additional carrot add about 1 minute.

FOOD FOR THOUGHT:
- 2 cups shredded carrots, packed
- ⅓ cup brown sugar, ⅓ cup butter
- ¾ cup chopped dates
- ¼ tsp. salt

Makes 5 servings.

Celery Almondine

3 Tbl. butter
1 rib celery, minced
¼ of a small onion, minced
3 Tbl. flour
½ tsp. salt
1 cup cream or evaporated milk

8 cups ½-inch-thick diagonally sliced celery
2 tsp. instant granular chicken bouillon

½ cup sour cream
⅔ cup slivered toasted almonds

In a suitable 2-cup utensil melt the butter (this will take about 20 seconds). Add celery and onion; mix to coat with butter. Cook covered about 1 minute 15 seconds or until tender. Stir in flour and salt; blend until smooth. Gradually stir in cream or milk. Cook 2 minutes 30 seconds to 3 minutes or until thickened; stir 2 to 3 times during cooking to keep mixture smooth. Cover and set aside.

Place the celery slices in a 1½-quart casserole or vegetable dish; sprinkle with the chicken bouillon. Cook covered about 7 minutes, until just crisp tender. Do not overcook. Drain. Stir in prepared sauce. Heat 2 minutes to 2 minutes 30 seconds. Stir in sour cream; sprinkle with toasted almonds.

Makes 6 servings.

If desired, substitute 1 can condensed cream of celery soup for the sauce. Decrease bouillon to 1 tsp. and add the ½ cup sour cream.

* * * * * * * * * *

To Toast Almonds:

Place almonds in 1 Tbl. butter or margarine in a small custard cup or other utensil. Cook 3 to 5 minutes, stirring occasionally, until toasted to desired degree.

Green Beans à la Nicoise

Zesty and flavorful!

1	package (10 oz.) frozen French cut green beans
¼	cup olive oil
1	tsp. salt
1	bay leaf
¼	tsp. ground cloves
1	medium onion, chopped
½	green pepper, chopped
2	tomatoes, cut in wedges

Place package of green beans in the microwave oven on a paper towel or plate. Cook 5 minutes, turning package over after 3 minutes. Set aside. In a 1-quart casserole or vegetable dish that is suitable for the microwave, combine olive oil, salt, cloves and bay leaf. Microwave 1 minute 30 seconds. Mix in cooked green beans, onion and pepper. Microwave covered about 4 minutes. Stir; add tomatoes, and cook covered an additional minute.

Makes 4 to 5 servings.

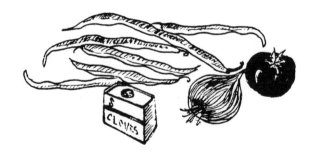

Fresh Green Beans 'n' Bacon

2 slices bacon
1 pound fresh green beans, cut in one-inch pieces
1 small onion, chopped
1 Tbl. water
½ tsp. salt
⅛ tsp. pepper

Dice bacon and place in a 1-quart suitable casserole. Cook covered 2 minutes 30 seconds to 3 minutes, stirring once or twice to keep pieces separated. Add green beans, onion, water, salt and pepper; stir to mix. Cook covered on 50% power 10 to 15 minutes, or until beans are tender. If your unit does not have variable power, cook on full power 5 minutes, let rest 5 minutes. Repeat the cook and rest cycle twice, cooking an additional 2 minutes if necessary. Stir once or twice during cooking for best results.

Makes 4 servings.

FOOD FOR THOUGHT:

To become tender, fresh green beans need slower cooking than most vegetables. Cooking on 50% power or the defrost cycle achieves this.

Herbed Onion Slices

Delicious with roast beef, meat loaf or burger steaks.

2	large onions, cut into ½-inch slices
3	Tbl. butter or margarine
1	Tbl. brown sugar
1	tsp. salt
⅛	tsp. pepper
½	tsp. sage
¼	cup finely minced celery
2	Tbl. finely chopped fresh parsley

In a small utensil combine all ingredients except onion slices. Cook until butter is melted and celery is crisp tender (this will take about 3 minutes). Place onion slices on a platter or other suitable utensil that can be used in the microwave oven. Divide herbed butter mixture equally among onion slices and spread over each. Cover with wax paper or loosely with plastic wrap; cook about 3 minutes 30 seconds or until onion is fork-tender.

Makes 6 servings.

Soy Onions

Especially good with barbecued meats.

2	large onions, sliced and separated into rings
2	Tbl. butter or margarine
1 to 2	Tbl. soy sauce

Place onions in a suitable utensil, dot with butter or margarine. Cook covered about 4 minutes; stir in soy sauce. Let stand approximately 3 minutes for flavor to be absorbed.

Makes 3 to 4 servings.

Summer Squash Crustless Quiche

1 pound summer squash
½ onion, thinly sliced
4 eggs, beaten
1½ cups grated Jack cheese
½ tsp. salt
½ tsp. each oregano and basil leaves, crushed between
    fingers to release flavors
⅛ tsp. pepper
2 Tbl. Italian seasoned bread crumbs
2 Tbl. Parmesan cheese
  Paprika

Slice and cook squash with the onion in a covered utensil that is suitable for the microwave oven, for about 6 minutes or until tender. Drain well. Beat eggs and stir in cheese. Mash squash, do not puree, and add to egg mixture; season. Pour into a lightly greased glass 9-inch pie plate. Mix together the bread crumbs and Parmesan cheese; distribute evenly over top of squash mixture in plate. Sprinkle with paprika. Cook 7 to 8 minutes, rotating dish 2 to 3 times during cooking. Cut into wedges to serve.

Makes 5 to 6 servings when served as a meal accompaniment.

FOOD FOR THOUGHT:

Summer squash varieties include zucchini, crookneck, and patty pan or scallop.

Baked Zucchini Frittata

Similar to a crustless quiche.

2   slices bacon, diced
¾   pound (4 small) zucchini, shredded or chopped fine
2   eggs
¾   cup cottage cheese
2   Tbl. Parmesan cheese
1   Tbl. flour
¼   tsp. anise seed, crushed
¼   tsp. salt
⅛   tsp. pepper
1   clove garlic, minced fine
¼   cup chopped fresh parsley, optional
¼   cup seasoned fine dry bread crumbs

* * * * * * * * * *

1   Tbl. Parmesan cheese, optional
     Paprika, optional

In an 8-inch pie plate cook the diced bacon, covered with a paper towel, for approximately 2 minutes. Stir halfway through the cooking time to separate pieces. Add zucchini and stir to mix in bacon and coat with drippings. Cook covered with wax paper 3 minutes. Meanwhile beat together the eggs, cheeses, flour, seasonings and bread crumbs. Pour over zucchini and mix well. Distribute mixture evenly in plate; sprinkle top with Parmesan cheese and lightly with paprika if desired. This will give better eye appeal! Cook about 5 minutes 30 seconds or until a knife comes out clean when inserted near the center. Let rest 5 minutes before cutting.

Makes 5 to 6 servings as a meal accompaniment; 3 servings as a main dish.

Zucchini Roma

½	cup saltine crackers, crushed fine
3	medium or 4 small zucchini, thinly sliced
1	small onion, thinly sliced
1	medium tomato, thinly sliced
½	tsp. salt
Scant ½	tsp. oregano, crushed
	Pepper to taste (about ⅛ tsp.)
¾	cup shredded Jack, Mozzarella or cheddar cheese

Layer ingredients except cheese in order given in a suitable 1½-quart utensil. Cook covered 5 to 6 minutes or until zucchini is fork-tender. Distribute cheese over top. If desired, cook an additional 45 seconds to melt cheese. However, generated heat will cause cheese to melt on standing.

Makes 4 servings.

* * * * * * * * * *

Special Spinach

A favorite of many.

2	packages (10 oz. each) frozen chopped spinach
1	cup sour cream
1	package of dry onion soup mix
1	tsp. Worcestershire sauce

Place spinach in the cartons in a glass utility dish or other suitable utensil (this is to catch moisture that will be released from spinach). Cook 7 minutes 30 seconds, turning packages over halfway through cooking time. When cool enough to handle, drain spinach well and squeeze out excess moisture. Combine sour cream, Worcestershire sauce and dry onion soup mix in a 1½-quart casserole; add spinach, mixing well. Cook covered 3 to 4 minutes or until hot through.

Makes 4 to 5 servings.

Tomato, Onion, Pepper Trio

A colorful combination!

2	medium green peppers, cut in chunks
1	medium onion, cut in half and slivered
½	tsp. sweet basil, crushed
1	tsp. salt, or more to taste
⅛	tsp. pepper
2	medium tomatoes, cut in wedges

Place green pepper and onion in a 1-quart casserole; sprinkle with ½ tsp. of the salt and the sweet basil. Stir to mix. Cook covered 4 minutes. Stir and top with tomato wedges; sprinkle with the remaining ½ tsp. salt and pepper. Cook an additional 2 to 3 minutes or until tomatoes are hot through.

Makes 4 servings.

* * * * * * * * * *

Vegetables Italiano

1	Tbl. olive oil
1	onion, slivered
1	green pepper, cut in 1-inch chunks
2	zucchini, cut in ¼-inch slices
⅛	tsp. garlic powder or 1 clove garlic, minced fine
½	tsp. Italian seasonings, crushed between fingers to release flavors
⅛	tsp. black pepper
2	tomatoes, cut in wedges

Place all ingredients except tomatoes in a 1-quart casserole or other suitable serving utensil; mix well. Cook covered 4 minutes. Add tomato wedges and stir gently to mix. Cook 3 minutes longer.

Makes 4 servings.

Baked Tomatoes

A good choice for that color you need at times on the dinner plate!

2   medium or large tomatoes
1   Tbl. butter or margarine
¼   cup seasoned bread crumbs
     Salt and pepper to taste
     Paprika

Cut tomatoes in half and place on a small dish that is suitable for the microwave oven. In a small dish like a custard cup place butter or margarine and bread crumbs. Cook about 20 seconds to melt butter or margarine; mix well. Salt and pepper tomato halves. Place 1 Tbl. crumb mixture on each half; sprinkle with paprika. Cook about 1 minute 30 seconds or until heated through.

Makes 4 servings.

A double recipe or 8 halves will cook in about 3 minutes 30 seconds to 4 minutes.

Baked Tomatoes Dijon

A tasty and colorful addition to the dinner plate!

        2   large tomatoes
            Salt and pepper to taste
        2   Tbl. mayonnaise
        2   tsp. Dijon mustard
        1   tsp. instant minced onion or 1 Tbl. fresh
            Paprika or fresh chopped parsley, optional

Cut tomatoes in half and place cut side up on a small dish that is suitable for the microwave oven. Sprinkle each half with salt and pepper. Mix together the mayonnaise, mustard and onion. Spread on tomato halves; sprinkle with paprika or chopped parsley if desired. Cook 1 minute 30 seconds to 2 minutes, or until hot through.

Makes 4 servings of one half each.

A double recipe will cook in 3 to 4 minutes.

FOOD FOR THOUGHT:

Time depends on size and beginning temperature of tomatoes!

Savory Cherry Tomatoes

3   small green onions, thinly sliced
1   Tbl. butter or margarine
½   tsp. basil, crushed, cumin, curry powder or dill weed
3   cups cherry tomatoes, stems removed
1   tsp. salt

In a utensil suitable for the microwave oven combine the onion, butter or margarine and desired seasoning; microwave 45 seconds or until butter or margarine is melted and onions are limp. Add tomatoes; sprinkle with salt. Cook uncovered 3 to 4 minutes, watching so that tomatoes do not burst but are warmed through.

Makes 4 servings.

No green onions??? Use 3 Tbl. finely chopped regular onion. It changes the flavor slightly, but it's still good!

Fresh Vegetable Medley

Fresh vegetables take on a new dimension when cooked in the microwave. Take note of their superb texture and color retention.

2	medium bunches of fresh broccoli (purchase about 1½ pounds)
2	small zucchini or crookneck squash
12	medium fresh mushrooms
1	small carrot
2 to 3	Tbl. butter, optional
2	small tomatoes, optional
	Seasoning to taste

Cut broccoli into flowerettes; save the stems for another use. Slice squash into ¼-inch thick slices; slice mushrooms or leave whole. Arrange vegetables on a platter suitable for the microwave, placing broccoli around outside edge and mushrooms in center. Tuck very thinly sliced carrots among the broccoli. Melt butter or margarine in a small custard cup or paper cup, if using (it will take about 20 seconds to melt); drizzle over vegetables and season lightly.

Cover with plastic wrap, sealing edges to keep in steam. (Note, no water is being added.) Microwave on full power 8 to 10 minutes, or until just crisp tender.

Remove plastic wrap carefully so as not to be burned by steam. Cut tomatoes into wedges, if using, and arrange over vegetables. Season tomatoes. Return to oven and microwave on full power 1 minute 30 seconds to 2 minutes or until tomatoes are heated through.

Makes 6 to 8 servings.

FOOD FOR THOUGHT:

It is important to slice the carrots thin so that they will become tender.

This medley is pictured on the cover!

Artichokes Monterey

2   9-ounce packages frozen artichoke hearts
2   Tbl. butter or margarine
2   Tbl. flour
1   tsp. instant granular chicken bouillon
½   tsp. salt
¼   tsp. white pepper
½   cup water
½   cup milk
1   Tbl. dry sherry
1   cup shredded Monterey Jack cheese
3   Tbl. dry bread crumbs

Place packages of artichoke hearts in the microwave oven on paper toweling. Microwave on full power 10 to 11 minutes, turning the packages over halfway through cooking time.

In a 1-quart casserole suitable for the microwave melt the butter or margarine (this will take about 20 seconds). Blend in flour, bouillon, salt and pepper. Stir in water and milk. Microwave about 4 minutes or until thick and bubbly, stirring frequently.

Add sherry and ¾ cup of the cheese, stirring until cheese melts. Drain artichokes and add to sauce. Microwave on full power about 3 minutes or until hot through. Sprinkle with remaining cheese that has been tossed with bread crumbs.

Makes 6 servings.

FOOD FOR THOUGHT:

If casserole has been made ahead and refrigerated, microwave on full power about 6 minutes, or on 50% power about 12 minutes, stirring once halfway through, then top with cheese and crumbs.

Bacon Bit Potatoes

An accompaniment made simple with the use of frozen hash browns and the microwave oven!

    1 package (12 oz.) frozen hash brown potatoes
    4 slices bacon, diced
    ½ cup chopped onion
       Salt and pepper to taste
    ½ cup shredded cheddar cheese

In package defrost potatoes on full power for 3 minutes; set aside. Cook bacon in a dish you will want to serve the potatoes from, and that is suitable for the microwave oven. Cook bacon covered with a paper towel 4 minutes 30 seconds to 4 minutes 45 seconds or until crisp. Stir one or two times during cooking to keep pieces separated. Remove bacon with a slotted spoon; set aside.

Reheat bacon fat for 40 seconds. Place onions in fat with potatoes on top. Season with salt and pepper. Cook covered 4 minutes. Stir to break up potatoes and continue cooking 3 minutes longer or until hot through. Mix in bacon bits. Top with shredded cheese.

Makes 4 servings.

* * * * * * * * * *

To double recipe:

Double amounts of ingredients. Defrost potatoes about 5 minutes. Cook bacon 7 minutes 30 seconds to 8 minutes. Reheat fat 1 minute. Cook completed casserole 5 minutes to 5 minutes 30 seconds; then an additional 3 minutes or until hot through.

For variation top with Parmesan cheese in place of cheddar cheese, decreasing amount to ¼ cup, or omit cheese entirely.

Baked Potatoes

Scrub potatoes and dry well. Pierce clear through with a sharp knife. Place on a double thickness of paper toweling (this absorbs some moisture) with at least one inch space between potatoes. If cooking a number of potatoes, place in a spoke fashion.

One medium-size potato will cook in about 5 minutes.
2 potatoes will cook in about 7 minutes,
3 in about 9 minutes, and
4 in about 12 minutes, and so on.
(see page 214)

Treat sweet potatoes in the same manner.

FOOD FOR THOUGHT:

For even cooking, try to choose potatoes of approximately the same size. If they are of different sizes it will probably be necessary to remove the smaller ones earlier.

If potatoes are of irregular shape, turning them over during microwave time will insure even cooking.

Placing potatoes on a paper towel-lined plate will aid in placing and removing a number of potatoes from the oven at one time.

To keep potatoes warm while cooking other foods, wrap them in a terry cloth towel. Terry cloth is absorbent and porous, allowing steam to escape, but will help retain their heat after cooking.

Sour Cream Herbed Potatoes

2 to 3   medium potatoes, diced
1   Tbl. water
½   cup sour cream
½   tsp. salt
⅛   tsp. garlic powder or 1 small clove garlic, minced fine
¼   tsp. oregano, crushed

Place potatoes and water in a casserole; stir. Cook covered 7 to 9 minutes or until tender. Stir once halfway through cooking. Mix together sour cream and seasonings; pour over potatoes and toss gently. Heat 1 to 2 minutes, stirring often. Watch carefully so that the sour cream does not curdle or separate.

Makes 3 to 4 servings.

* * * * * * * * * *

Potatoes Gralita

Another easy but good recipe!

3   cups (one-half of a 24-oz. package) frozen potatoes O'Brien*
1   can condensed cream of celery soup, undiluted
½   cup sour cream
1   tsp. salt
  Paprika

In a 1-quart casserole mix all ingredients together except paprika. Cook covered 12 to 15 minutes, stirring occasionally. Sprinkle with paprika before serving.

Makes 4 servings.

If recipe is doubled cook 16 to 20 minutes.

Paprika enhances the appearance!

*Potatoes O'Brien are diced potatoes with chopped onions and peppers.

Easy Orange Glazed Potatoes

3   medium-size sweet potatoes, cooked, peeled and cut in
    ½-inch slices OR use canned sweet potatoes that are
    well drained
¼   cup orange marmalade
2   Tbl. butter
    Salt to taste
⅛   tsp. ground ginger, optional

If using fresh sweet potatoes, pierce clear through with a sharp knife and place on paper toweling in the microwave oven. Have a space of at least one inch between potatoes. Cook about 9 minutes or until tender (can be easily pierced with a fork). Let cool enough to handle and peel. Cut into ½ to ¾-inch slices and place into a casserole dish. Melt butter in a small suitable utensil (this will take about 20 seconds); mix in marmalade, salt and ginger if using. Spoon over potatoes and stir gently. Cook uncovered 4 minutes; stir again and serve. If made ahead and refrigerated add about 1 minute 15 seconds microwave time and stir once during heating.

Makes 4 to 5 servings.

A garnish of orange slices and sprigs of fresh parsley are in order here!

Super Sweets

An unusual combo of sweet potatoes and apricots. My students who said they normally don't care for sweet potatoes loved this recipe.

2	fresh sweet potatoes to equal one pound, or 1 can (16 oz.) sweet potatoes, well drained
1	can (16 oz.) apricot halves, well drained
½	(reserve ½ cup syrup)
½	cup pecan halves
¾	cup sugar
1½	tsp. cornstarch
¼	tsp. each salt and ground ginger
1 to 2	tsp. fresh grated orange peel
2	Tbl. butter or margarine

If using fresh sweet potatoes, pierce clear through with a sharp knife and place on a paper towel in the microwave oven with a space of at least one inch between them. Cook 7 to 9 minutes or until easily pierced with a fork. Let cool enough to handle and peel. Cut into thick slices and place in a 6 × 10-inch glass baking dish or other suitable utensil. Place apricot halves over sweet potato slices. Distribute pecan halves over top.

In a medium-size bowl or utensil make a sauce with the reserved ½ cup syrup, sugar, cornstarch, salt, ginger and orange peel. Cook until mixture boils and is thickened (this will take about 4 minutes). Add butter or margarine and stir until melted; pour sauce overall. Cook uncovered about 8 minutes or until hot and bubbly. If made ahead and refrigerated, cook about 12 minutes.

Makes 6 to 8 servings.

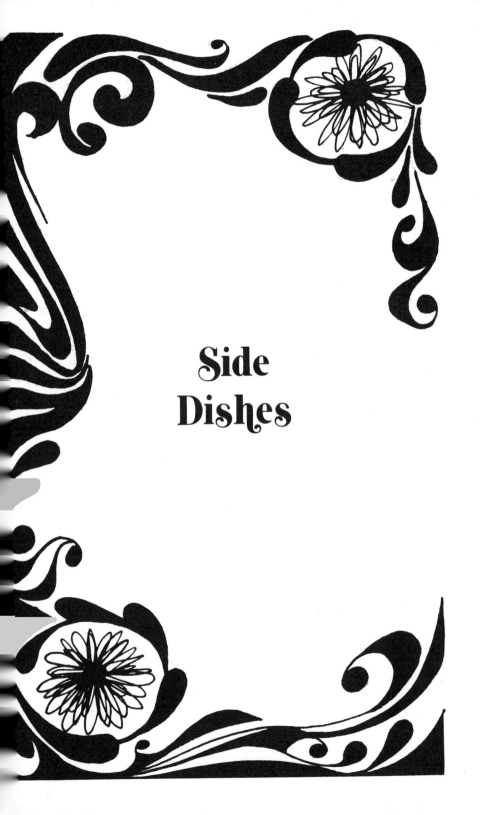

Side
Dishes

Buttered Noodles

   3   cups water
   1   Tbl. salt
   1   package (8 oz.) medium noodles
   3   Tbl. butter or margarine
      Salt to taste
      Poppy seeds or chopped fresh parsley, optional

In a 1½ to 2-quart utensil heat water to boiling (this will take about 10 minutes). Add 1 Tbl. salt and noodles; stir. Cook 4 minutes or until tender, stirring two to three times during cooking to keep noodles from sticking together. Drain well. Add seasonings to taste; stir in butter until melted.

Makes 5 servings.

****

Apple Sauce Noodle Casserole

Excellent with poultry or pork. A favorite of my family!

   3   cups water
   1   Tbl. salt
   1   package (8 oz.) wide noodles
   ¼   cup butter or margarine, optional
   1   can (16 oz. or 2 cups) apple sauce
   ¼   cup sugar
   1   tsp. cinnamon

To cook noodles bring 3 cups water to a boil in a 1½ to 2-quart utensil (this will take about 10 minutes). Add 1 Tbl. salt and noodles; cook 4 minutes or until tender. Stir two to three times during cooking to keep noodles from sticking together. Drain well. Place cooked noodles in a casserole and stir in remaining ingredients. If desired dot top with extra butter; sprinkle with additional cinnamon and sugar. Cook 6 to 7 minutes or until hot and bubbly.

Makes 4 to 5 servings.

Rice with Almonds

2   cups cooked rice (instructions follow)
2   Tbl. oil
1   small onion, chopped
½   green pepper, chopped (optional)
⅛   tsp. garlic powder or 1 clove garlic, finely minced
½   tsp. salt
¼   tsp. pepper
2   Tbl. soy sauce
½   cup slivered or sliced almonds
3   Tbl. chopped fresh parsley

Prepare rice as follows or use leftover rice. In a 1½-quart casse- *cook longer* role combine ¾ cup regular long grain rice, 1½ cups water and ½ tsp. salt. Cook covered 11 to 12 minutes, or until most of the water has been absorbed. Stir and let stand covered 5 minutes to allow remaining liquid to be fully absorbed. Fluff with a fork. Set aside.

In a small bowl suitable for the microwave oven cook onion, green pepper if using, garlic, salt and pepper in oil for approximately 3 minutes. Stir into rice along with soy sauce and almonds; cook 1 minute 30 seconds. If using cold rice, cook about 3 minutes 30 seconds or until heated through. Garnish with chopped fresh parsley, if desired.

Makes 4 servings.

FOOD FOR THOUGHT:
Refrigerated rice reheats at about 1 minute 30 seconds per cup.

Chile Cheese Rice Casserole

1½	cups cooked rice
1 to 1½	cups sour cream
¼	cup chopped green chiles or to taste
½	cup sliced stuffed green or ripe olives
1	cup (4 oz.) shredded mild cheese (I like to use Jack cheese)
	Salt and pepper
½	cup shredded cheddar cheese for topping
	Paprika
2 to 3	sliced green onions

In a 1-quart casserole cook ½ cup rice in 1 cup water and ½ tsp. salt for approximately 11 minutes, covered. Let stand 5 minutes to absorb liquid fully. Fluff with a fork. Mix in sour cream, chiles, sliced olives, 1 cup shredded mild cheese, salt and pepper to taste. Cook covered 3 to 5 minutes or until hot through. Top with cheddar cheese and sprinkle with paprika.

Let stand covered as long as 10 minutes before serving. During this time the cheese topping will melt. Garnish with green onion slices.

FOOD FOR THOUGHT:

This dish is good served with barbecued chicken, or include in a Mexican foods menu!

Confetti Rice

A colorful accompaniment to most meats or poultry!

1	cup regular long grain rice
¼	cup minced green pepper
¼	cup minced onion
¼	cup butter or margarine
1	tsp. salt
2	cups water
¼	cup diced pimiento

Combine all ingredients, except pimiento, in a 2-quart casserole or other suitable utensil. Cook covered 12 to 14 minutes or until most of the water has been absorbed by the rice. Stir in pimiento, cover and let stand 5 minutes or longer for water to be absorbed fully. Fluff with a fork and adjust seasonings before serving.

Makes 4 to 5 servings.

If your microwave oven has variable power you can cook the rice on full power 5 minutes, reduce the power setting to 50% and continue cooking 10 to 12 minutes longer or until all liquid is absorbed and rice is tender. Then proceed as above.

FOOD FOR THOUGHT:

Rice reheats nicely!

One cup refrigerated rice heats in about 1 minute 30 seconds on full power. Add about 1 minute for each additional cup, stirring occasionally.

Parslied Rice

1 cup rice
2 cups water
1 tsp. salt
¼ cup butter or margarine
¼ cup fresh chopped parsley

In a 2 to 2½-quart casserole, combine the rice, water and salt. Add butter or margarine. Cover and cook 12 to 14 minutes on full power. Stir; let stand covered at least 5 minutes, or see page 105. Add parsley and fluff with a fork before serving.

Makes 4 to 6 servings.

FOOD FOR THOUGHT:

For plain cooked rice, just eliminate the butter or margarine and parsley.

1 cup raw rice yields 3 cups cooked.

Simple Rice Casserole

1	cup regular long grain rice
½	tsp. salt
2	tsp. instant granular bouillon (chicken, beef, or vegetable)
2	Tbl. instant minced onion or ¼ cup fresh minced onion
2	cups water
2	Tbl. butter or margarine
	Chopped fresh parsley, optional

Combine all ingredients except parsley in a 2-quart casserole. Stir well. Cook covered 12 to 14 minutes. Let stand 5 minutes to allow liquid to be absorbed fully. Fluff with a fork before serving. Garnish with chopped parsley if desired.

Makes 4 to 5 servings.

If your microwave oven has variable power you can cook on full power 5 minutes, reduce power setting to 50% and cook 10 to 12 minutes longer or until all liquid is absorbed. Fluff with a fork before serving.

A large utensil is necessary when cooking rice to allow room for boilup!

Spaghetti with Sautéed Mushrooms in Garlic Butter

    8   ounces spaghetti or linguine, cooked
    ¼   cup butter
    1   clove garlic, finely minced
         Salt to taste
    ½   pound fresh mushrooms, sliced

In a serving dish large enough to hold prepared spaghetti, and that is suitable for the microwave oven, melt butter; add garlic, mushrooms and salt. Stir to coat mushrooms with butter. Cook 1 minute 30 seconds to 2 minutes. Toss together with cooked spaghetti; cook an additional minute or until hot through.

Makes about 4 servings.

This is delicious served with CHICKEN PARMESAN; recipe is on page 61.

FOOD FOR THOUGHT:
Clean mushrooms by rinsing under cold water quickly; drain well. Never soak mushrooms in water!

* * * * * * * * * *

To Prepare Spaghetti in the Microwave:
In a 7½ × 11¾ × 2-inch dish, heat 3 cups water 8 to 10 minutes or until boiling. Add spaghetti; stir to separate. Cook about 8 minutes, stirring every 2 minutes. Let stand 5 minutes or until tender. Rinse and drain well.

FOOD FOR THOUGHT:
1 pound uncooked spaghetti makes 6 to 8 servings.

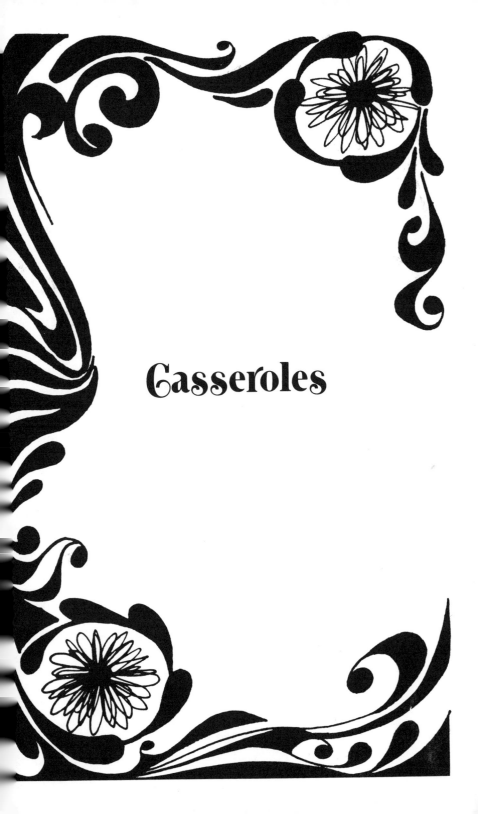

Casseroles

CASSEROLES

Casseroles are of interest to most cooks and their families. They usually can be easily converted to microwave cooking.

For microwave timing, a general rule of thumb is about one-fourth of the conventional cooking time. Consider density, beginning temperature of ingredients involved, and mass or volume. Logically, denser items will take longer to cook as will extremely cold ingredients. Also, additional cooking time is needed when you add more volume to the oven. An example is, if a casserole is to bake for one hour conventionally, it will cook in approximately 15 minutes in the microwave. Since it is always best to undercook, check after 12 minutes of cooking time; however, it could take 17 minutes or more.

Because evaporation is minimal in microwave cooking, it is sometimes necessary to reduce liquids slightly. For instance, if one cup of liquid is called for in a regular recipe, try reducing it to ¾ cup in the microwave adaptation. However, if uncooked rice or pasta is being prepared, the regular amount of liquid is still necessary for rehydration or for the rice or pasta to become tender.

Cheese should be placed on top of casserole dishes towards the end or after cooking is completed. This prevents the cheese from toughening. Generated heat from the casserole will allow the cheese to melt while standing for a few minutes. For crispness to be retained, toppings such as dry or toasted bread crumbs should be sprinkled on after cooking is finished.

A covering of wax paper will help casserole dishes retain even heat, but it allows some moisture or steam to escape. In some instances a tight-fitting cover is necessary for moisture retention; use a casserole lid or plastic wrap covering.

Through experience you will discover whether or not rotation of utensils is required in your microwave oven. To insure even cooking, stirring or rearranging of food is often beneficial or necessary. When stirring is impossible or undesirable, rotation of the utensil is advisable.

If your microwave oven has a variable power feature, you have the option to lower the power setting for slower and more even cooking, often reducing the need to stir or to rotate.

Beefy Chowder

A thick soup-like casserole that is a quick and economical one-dish meal!

½	pound lean ground beef
1	cup uncooked shell or elbow macaroni
1	small onion, chopped
1	cup (8 oz. can) tomato sauce
1	cup water
1	can (7 oz.) whole kernel corn, undrained
½	medium green pepper, chopped
½	cup diced celery
1	tsp. salt
⅛	tsp. pepper
⅛	tsp. garlic powder
1½ to 2	tsp. chili powder

In a 2-quart casserole suitable for the microwave oven, crumble the ground beef. Stir in the remaining ingredients, trying not to break up the meat too much. Cook covered on full power 15 minutes to 16 minutes 30 seconds, stirring after 8 minutes of cooking time. Let stand 5 minutes; stir again. Serve in soup bowls.

Makes 4 servings.

FOOD FOR THOUGHT:

A large utensil is necessary, as the pasta will cause the mixture to boil up, and you'll be surprised how far only ½ pound of ground meat will go.

The only accompaniments needed for this meal are a tossed green salad, possibly garlic cheese bread, and for dessert. . . how about APPLE PIE? See page 148.

Crêpes Ensenada

Flour or corn tortillas replace the conventional crêpe, giving these a Mexican influence.

8	small (7-inch diameter) flour or corn tortillas
8	thin slices ham
½	pound Jack cheese, cut into 8 equal sticks
¼	of a canned green chile per crêpe
	Crêpe sauce, recipe follows

Crêpe Sauce:

3	Tbl. butter or margarine
3	Tbl. flour
2	tsp. instant granular chicken bouillon
¼	tsp. ground cumin
1¼	cups milk
¼	cup sour cream
3	Tbl. dry sherry
1	can (2¼ oz.) sliced ripe olives, well drained
	Paprika
2	green onions, thinly sliced or chopped

In a small utensil suitable for the microwave oven melt the butter or margarine; blend in the flour, bouillon and cumin. Stir in milk. Microwave 5 minutes, stirring frequently. Blend in sour cream and sherry. Fold in olives and set aside.

Soften tortillas, see below. Place a slice of ham on each tortilla and top with a chile strip and stick of cheese. Roll up and place seam side down in a 7½ × 11¾-inch glass utility dish, slightly separated. Pour sauce overall. Sprinkle with paprika. Microwave on full power about 12 minutes or until hot through. Garnish with sliced or chopped green onions. Makes 4 servings.

FOOD FOR THOUGHT:

See page 177 for softening flour tortillas. When using corn tortillas, for easier rolling and to prevent cracking, brush each lightly with oil; place on a dish and cover with wax paper. Microwave about 2 minutes or until hot.

Quick Cassoulet

A hearty casserole which is a true favorite!

3	cans (16 oz. each) white beans, drained
¾	pound hot Italian sausages, casings removed
4 to 5	slices bacon, cut in pieces
¾	pound lamb (about 3 lamb chops), cubed
¾	pound pork (about 3 pork chops), cubed
1	large onion, chopped
3	cloves garlic, minced
	Salt and pepper to taste
2	Tbl. chili sauce, tomato sauce, or catsup
½	tsp. thyme
¼	cup chopped fresh parsley
1	large bay leaf
½ to 1	cup soft fresh bread crumbs
	Fresh chopped parsley for garnish, optional
	Paprika, optional

In a large casserole place the drained beans and set aside. In a medium-size cooking utensil, microwave the sausage, covered with a paper towel, for 5 to 5 minutes 30 seconds or until done. Remove cooked sausage and set aside to cool. Discard drippings.

Cook bacon pieces in the same utensil 4 to 5 minutes, covered with paper toweling, stirring once or twice. (Bacon should not be crisp.) Remove bacon with a slotted spoon and add to beans in casserole. Reserve drippings in utensil, reheating approximately 45 seconds. Add cubed lamb, pork, chopped onion, garlic, salt and pepper. Mix well. Microwave covered with paper toweling 9 minutes, stirring once or twice.

While meats are cooking, cut sausages in chunks or thick slices; add to beans. To the meat mixture add chili sauce, tomato sauce or catsup, thyme, parsley and bay leaf. Stir to blend and cook an additional 2 minutes. Combine the meat mixture and the bean mixture. Mix well. Microwave 10 minutes covered or until hot and bubbly. Top with fresh bread crumbs and cook uncovered 5 minutes longer.

Sprinkle the top with paprika and additional chopped parsley, if desired, for added eye appeal.

Makes 6 to 8 servings.

FOOD FOR THOUGHT:
If made ahead and refrigerated before serving, do not add bread crumbs. Reheat, covered, on full power 15 minutes, stirring once or twice. Uncover; add bread crumbs, etc., and proceed as above.

Manicotti

An Italian favorite made easy! A medium power setting is necessary.

¾	pound lean ground beef
3	cans (8 oz. each) tomato sauce
1	cup water
1	Tbl. Italian seasonings
1½	tsp. salt
¼	tsp. garlic powder or 1 large clove garlic, finely minced

* * * * * * * * * *

8 uncooked manicotti shells

For the sauce, crumble ground beef in a large casserole dish; microwave covered with paper toweling 5 minutes, stirring twice during cooking. Add tomato sauce, water and seasonings. Cook covered with wax paper 10 minutes, stirring 2 to 3 times. Meanwhile stuff 8 uncooked manicotti shells with the following mixture:

¾	pound ricotta cheese
2	Tbl. fresh minced parsley
1	egg, beaten
1	cup (4 oz.) shredded or grated Mozzarella cheese
3	Tbl. grated Parmesan cheese

Pour about 1 cup of the sauce in the bottom of a 7½ × 11¾-inch glass utility dish. Place stuffed shells on top. Pour remaining sauce overall, making sure sauce goes between shells. Cover with plastic wrap and cook 5 minutes on full power; reduce power to 50% or simmer and microwave 25 minutes.

It is usually necessary to redistribute sauce over manicotti; in doing so, remove plastic wrap carefully so as not to be burned by the steam.

Let rest 10 minutes, covered with plastic wrap or wax paper. Sprinkle with additional Parmesan cheese before serving.

Makes 4 servings of 2 manicotti per serving.

114

Quick and Easy Sausage Dinner Casserole

1   roll (12 oz.) pork sausage
1   can condensed cream of celery soup, undiluted
¾   cup milk
½   cup chopped onion
⅛   tsp. pepper
½   tsp. salt
1   cup quick cooking rice (uncooked)
1½ cups sliced celery
1   cup (4 oz.) shredded cheddar cheese

In a 1½-quart casserole break up sausage; microwave for 6 minutes, stirring once or twice. Drain off fat; add remaining ingredients, except cheese. Microwave covered 10 minutes. Top with cheese and let stand 3 to 5 minutes for cheese to melt.

Makes 4 to 5 servings.

* * * * * * * * * *

Spicy Sausage with Shell Macaroni

1   pound Italian sausage (casings removed), cut in
     ¼-inch slices
2   cans (16 oz. each) tomatoes, chopped (not drained)
¼   cup water
½   cup minced onion
2   cloves garlic, minced
½   tsp. salt
     pepper to taste
2   tsp. oregano, crushed
1   tsp. sweet basil, crushed
1   tsp. sugar
2   cups small shell macaroni, uncooked

Mix all ingredients together in a 2-quart casserole. Microwave covered about 16 minutes or until macaroni is tender. Stir twice during cooking to keep macaroni from sticking and ingredients mixed. Let stand 5 minutes before serving. Top with Parmesan cheese, if desired. Makes 4 to 5 servings.

Rumaki Casserole

If you're fond of the popular Rumaki appetizer, you'll like this casserole version of mine!

1 to 1¼	pounds chicken livers
¼	cup soy sauce
½	tsp. salt or to taste
⅛	tsp. pepper
¼	tsp. garlic powder or 1 large clove garlic, minced fine
½	tsp. paprika
½	tsp. Gravy Master or Kitchen Bouquet optional, but helps give the dish better color)
1	Tbl. flour
¼	pound bacon
1	can (8 oz.) water chestnuts
	Chopped fresh parsley for garnish, optional

Drain chicken livers and cut into medium-size pieces, removing any fatty tissue. Mix with soy sauce, salt, pepper, garlic, paprika, browning agent and flour. Marinate while cutting up and cooking bacon.

To prepare bacon, cut into 1-inch pieces and place in a 1½-quart casserole. Microwave, covered with paper toweling, about 5 minutes or until just barely crisp. Stir occasionally to keep pieces separated.

Meanwhile, slice water chestnuts and set aside. When bacon is done, remove from casserole dish. Reheat drippings 1 to 2 minutes; add chicken liver mixture to hot drippings. Cover with wax paper and cook 10 to 12 minutes, stirring once or twice. Add remaining ingredients and cook an additional 3 minutes. Garnish with chopped fresh parsley if desired.

Makes 4 servings.

* * * * * * * * * *

Serving suggestions on next page.

Serve RUMAKI CASSEROLE with hot PARSLIED RICE (recipe is on page 104), butter sauced peas, and cucumber salad garnished with sesame seeds.

* * * * * * * * * *

RUMAKI CASSEROLE can also be served as an hors d'oeuvre. Use toothpicks to spear the chicken livers and water chestnuts.

Quiches also make delightful main dishes and appetizers. Recipes for a few are indexed.

* * * * * * * * * *

The following appetizer recipes make good main dishes:

ORIENTAL MEATBALLS, page 24
MEATBALLS OLÉ, page 23
MEATBALLS IN WINE SAUCE, page 26

117

Grace's Poor Man's Stroganoff

1 pound lean ground beef
1 Tbl. flour
1 Tbl. paprika
¾ tsp. salt
¼ tsp. pepper
1 envelope dry mushroom soup mix
1 medium onion, slivered
1 cup sliced celery (about 2 ribs)
1 cup sliced fresh mushrooms (about 3 oz.)
1 cup sour cream
3 cups hot cooked rice

In a 1½-quart casserole crumble beef. Sprinkle with flour, paprika, salt and pepper. Mix slightly. Microwave covered with paper toweling 5 minutes, stirring once. Add dry soup mix, onion and celery, mixing well. Cook covered 4 to 5 minutes until vegetables are just crisp tender. Add mushrooms; stir and cook covered 4 minutes longer. Just before serving stir in sour cream; heat an additional minute.

Serve over hot cooked rice.

Makes 4 to 5 servings.

FOOD FOR THOUGHT:

Do not boil after adding sour cream or mixture will separate. If sour cream is at room temperature, there's no need to heat further after stirring in.

If desired, in place of soup mix increase flour to 2 Tbl., salt to 2 tsp., and pepper to ½ tsp. Add 1 small clove garlic, minced fine, then proceed as directed.

Quick and Easy Tamale Pie

With a tossed green salad and a dessert, this is a complete meal.

Crust:

1¼	cups cold water
1	tsp. salt
1	tsp. chili powder
½	cup cornmeal

Combine all ingredients in a 1-quart utensil suitable for the microwave. Cook about 4 minutes or until thick and stiff, stirring frequently. Line the sides and bottom of a lightly buttered casserole or 10-inch pie plate with mixture.

Filling:

1¾	cups (15 oz. can) chili con carne
½	cup chopped green pepper
½	cup chopped onion
½	cup (2¼ oz. can) sliced ripe olives, drained
½	cup whole kernel corn, drained
1	tsp. salt
⅛	tsp. garlic powder

* * * * * * * * * *

1	cup shredded cheddar cheese

Mix all ingredients together, except cheese. Fill crust with mixture. Microwave covered with wax paper 6 minutes to 7 minutes 30 seconds. Distribute cheese over top and let stand 2 to 3 minutes for cheese to melt.

Makes 4 to 5 servings.

Zesty Zucchini and Noodle Casserole

        1   package (8 oz.) wide noodles
        3   cups water
        1   Tbl. salt

                        * * * * * * * * * *

        1   pound lean ground beef
       ½   of a small onion, chopped
       ½   of a small green pepper, finely chopped
        3   cups (about ¾ pound) zucchini, cut in small chunks
        2   tsp. salt or to taste
       ¼   tsp. *each* oregano and basil leaves, crushed
        1   jar (16 oz.) spaghetti sauce, preferably extra thick
        1   cup (about 3 oz.) lightly packed, sliced fresh
              mushrooms
  OR 1   can (4 oz.) mushrooms, well drained
        1   cup (4 oz.) shredded cheddar cheese
       ⅓   cup grated Parmesan cheese

In a 1½ to 2½-quart utensil that is suitable for the microwave bring the water to a boil (this will take about 10 minutes). Stir in salt and noodles. Cook on full power 3 minutes or until not quite tender; rinse, drain and set aside.

In a 3-quart casserole crumble the ground beef; stir in onion and green pepper. Cook covered with wax paper about 4 minutes or until meat is just slightly pink, stirring after 2 minutes of cooking. Drain off excess grease. Stir in zucchini, salt, oregano and basil. Continue cooking covered with wax paper 5 minutes or until zucchini is crisp tender. Add sauce, mushrooms, cooked noodles and cheeses, stirring to mix. Microwave on full power 5 to 6 minutes or until hot through.
Makes 6 to 8 servings.

FOOD FOR THOUGHT:

If desired additional cheddar cheese may be sprinkled on top of the casserole after cooking. Let stand a few minutes for the cheese to melt.

A simple tossed salad and dessert makes this a complete meal.

Eggs

EGGS

Timing is very important when cooking eggs in the microwave oven. If overcooked, they are tough and rubbery. Scrambled eggs give best results, but poached and baked eggs can be done successfully.

Internal pressure can cause eggs to burst, so it is advisable to prick the yolk before cooking. If you do it carefully (go straight down and up) you will not break the yolk.

Never cook eggs in their shell in the microwave oven.

Huevos Enchiladas

Spicy scrambled eggs with tortillas, great for that special breakfast or brunch.

4   eggs
⅓   cup cottage cheese
    Salt to taste
4   snack-size (7-inch diameter) flour tortillas
1   can (7 oz.) green chile salsa
1   cup (4 oz.) shredded cheddar cheese
    Avocado slices
    Sliced green onion, optional

Beat together in a 1-quart bowl or other utensil suitable for the microwave oven the eggs, cottage cheese, and salt. Cook 3 minutes 30 seconds to 4 minutes, stirring once during cooking and after cooking. Eggs should be cooked but soft. Divide equally and spoon onto the tortillas. Roll up and place seam side down in a dish that has a small amount of salsa on the bottom, about 3 Tbl. Pour remaining salsa over top and sprinkle cheese down the center. Heat in the microwave about 2 minutes 30 seconds to 3 minutes or until cheese is melted and enchiladas are heated through.

Garnish with avocado slices and sliced green onions.

Makes 4 servings.

FOOD FOR THOUGHT:

To make 6 servings use 6 eggs, ½ cup cottage cheese, 6 tortillas, 1½ cans salsa and 1¼ cups shredded cheese. Microwave eggs about 4 minutes 30 seconds. Heat enchiladas about 4 minutes 15 seconds.

Good accompaniments would be STEWED FRUIT MEDLEY, SPICY SAUSAGE RING, or BACON (recipes are indexed), and additional warm tortillas with butter.

Individual Omelets

The versatile omelet can be a simple or elaborate affair. Be adventuresome!

    3   eggs
    3   Tbl. water
        Salt and pepper to taste
    1   Tbl. butter or margarine

Melt butter or margarine in a 9-inch glass or ceramic pie plate (this will take 15 to 20 seconds). Beat eggs well with water and seasonings. Spread melted butter or margarine over bottom of dish and add egg mixture. Microwave 1 minute 45 seconds. With a spatula lift outer edges and allow uncooked portion to flow to outside edges; cook an additional minute. Place filling down center, fold and slip onto serving plate. Garnish with additional filling.

I find it advantageous to cover the dish with a paper plate. This helps hold in the heat and the omelet will cook more evenly.

For a two-egg omelet: use 2 eggs and 2 Tbl. water. Proceed as above but use a 7 or 8-inch plate; cook 1 minute 15 seconds, then an additional 45 seconds.

Fillings are too numerous to count. Listed are a few suggestions:

    Seasoned mushrooms or
    Green pepper and onion,
    Chopped ham,
    Shredded cheese,
    Diced chiles and cheese,
    Potato and bacon,
    Jam or jelly, and so on.

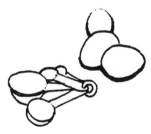

Jack Cheese Casserole Omelet

  8   eggs
  1   cup milk
  3   Tbl. diced green chiles or to taste
  4   green onions, thinly sliced, or ¼ cup minced onion
  1   tsp. seasoned salt
2½ cups shredded Jack cheese

In a 1-quart casserole (fairly straight-sided) or a soufflé dish, beat eggs well. Stir in milk, seasoned salt, chiles, onion and all but ½ cup cheese. Microwave about 11 minutes or until mixture is set. Halfway through cooking time, lift the outer edges of the egg mixture to allow the uncooked portion to flow to the outside edges.

When omelet is cooked, top with remaining ½ cup cheese and sprinkle with additional green onions and paprika, if desired. Or sprinkle with additional seasoned salt. Let stand 3 to 5 minutes before serving, to allow cheese topping to melt and omelet to firm up further.

Makes 4 to 5 servings.

FOOD FOR THOUGHT:

One-half of the recipe, or 4 eggs, cooks in about 6 minutes.

If you feel slower cooking would be beneficial and you have a variable power unit, microwave on full power for the first 3 minutes, then lower the power setting, allowing additional time for the slower cooking.

Scrambled Eggs

You'll find greater volume in microwave-scrambled eggs.

    6 eggs
    6 Tbl. milk or water (I prefer water for fluffy eggs)
       Salt and pepper to taste
    2 Tbl. butter or margarine, optional

In a bowl, casserole, or suitable serving dish, melt butter or margarine. (Or spray with a vegetable coating.) Add eggs and water or milk and seasonings and beat well. Microwave 3 minutes 30 seconds. Stir; cook 1 minute to 1 minute 30 seconds longer. At this point eggs will be soufflé-like; stir to scramble.

For an individual serving of two eggs, melt 1 Tbl. butter or margarine in a soup or cereal bowl, or spray with vegetable coating. Beat in eggs and 2 Tbl. milk or water with seasonings. Microwave 1 minute 15 seconds; stir and cook 30 to 45 seconds longer. Stir again and serve.

FOOD FOR THOUGHT:

Eggs will cook at slightly different rates of speed because of size or beginning temperature. Also, personal preference will help determine the total cooking time. Remember, eggs do continue to cook after removing from the oven because of generated heat. Do not overcook!

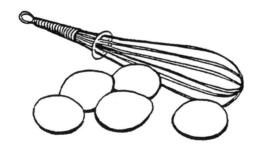

Cheese Soufflé

The beauty of a soufflé is fleeting, so take it directly to the table and be ready to eat it without delay. Slow cooking is a necessity!

3 Tbl. butter or margarine
3 Tbl. flour
¾ cup evaporated milk
1 tsp. instant granular chicken bouillon
⅛ tsp. cayenne
⅛ tsp. dry mustard
½ tsp. salt
½ cup finely shredded cheddar cheese
3 eggs, separated
¼ tsp. cream of tartar
Paprika

In a large utensil suitable for the microwave oven, melt the butter or margarine (this will take about 25 seconds). Blend in flour and seasonings; gradually stir in milk. Cook 3 minutes or until thickened, stirring 2 to 3 times to keep the mixture smooth. Add cheese; stir until melted. Beat the egg yolks and add to mixture. Whip egg whites until frothy; add cream of tartar, continuing to beat until stiff but not dry. Fold into cheese mixture. Pour into an ungreased 1-quart or 7-inch soufflé dish. Sprinkle top lightly with paprika.

Cook on 50% power 11 to 12 minutes or until soufflé looks firm and is well-puffed. Serve immediately.

Makes 3 to 4 servings.

FOOD FOR THOUGHT:

Evaporated milk makes the best soufflés in the microwave oven. Regular milk may be used, but the soufflé tends to fall more rapidly after removing from the oven.

Quiche Lorraine

You might know this as a Cheese and Bacon Pie; by either name it's a gourmet's delight.

	Pastry for a 9-inch pie
1	cup (4 oz.) shredded Swiss, Gruyère, or Jarlsberg cheese
2	Tbl. flour
¼	cup finely chopped onion
6	slices bacon, cooked and crumbled
4	eggs
1	cup half and half or evaporated milk, scalded
½	tsp. salt
¼	tsp. pepper
⅛	tsp. cayenne or a drop or two of hot pepper sauce
	Paprika
	Chopped fresh parsley, optional

See page 142 on pies. Use the recipe for pastry on page 151 or your favorite recipe. Ease dough into a glass or ceramic pie plate or quiche dish. Microwave on full power 4 to 5 minutes or until no longer doughy. Set aside to cool.

Toss together the cheese and flour; distribute over crust. Top with onion and bacon. Beat eggs well with salt, pepper and cayenne. Gradually stir in hot milk. Pour egg mixture overall. Sprinkle top with paprika and parsley, if using.

Microwave on 50% power (the same as defrost or medium setting on some models) 15 to 17 minutes or until filling is set. Halfway through the cooking time rotate the dish and cover with wax paper. Let stand 5 to 10 minutes. In this time the filling will continue to firm up. Serve warm or at room temperature.

Makes 5 sizable servings.

FOOD FOR THOUGHT:

The wax paper holds in some of the heat, resulting in a shorter cooking time.

It will take approximately 2 minutes to scald one cup of milk.

Shrimp or Tuna Quiche

A good luncheon dish, or serve as an appetizer!

1	8-inch pie shell
1	Tbl. flour

* * * * * * * * * *

1½	cups shredded Swiss, Jarlsberg or Jack cheese (my favorite is Jack)
½	cup finely chopped onion
1	can (6 oz.) shrimp or tuna, well drained
2	eggs
1	small can (5.33 oz. or ⅔ cup) evaporated milk
1	Tbl. lemon juice
¾	tsp. seasoned salt
	Paprika and chopped fresh parsley

Make your favorite pie crust recipe or use a commercially frozen pie shell. Place in either a glass or ceramic pie plate. Microwave for 3 minutes 30 seconds to 4 minutes or until no longer doughy. Set aside to cool.

When cool, sprinkle 1 Tbl. flour or dry bread crumbs over bottom of crust (this helps prevent a soggy crust). Evenly distribute over the bottom the cheese, shrimp or tuna, and onion. Beat eggs together with evaporated milk, lemon juice and seasoned salt. Pour over ingredients in dish. Sprinkle with paprika and fresh chopped parsley.

Cook on full power about 9 minutes, rotating the dish three times during cooking. Or you may use a reduced power setting of 70% and cook about 12 minutes or until filling is almost set in center. Let rest for 5 minutes before serving; in this time it will continue to firm up.

Makes 3 to 4 servings.

FOOD FOR THOUGHT:

The paprika and chopped parsley give the quiche good eye appeal and color!

If using frozen cooked shrimp, defrost and drain well before distributing over cheese in crust.

129

Egg Foo Young Casserole

An easy casserole version of the popular Chinese pancakes. Great for brunch, lunch or a light supper!

2 Tbl. oil
2 cups (about ¼ pound) fresh bean sprouts,
    coarsely chopped
⅓ cup thinly sliced green onions, including tops
⅓ cup (about 1 large rib) celery, finely chopped
    Salt and pepper to taste
6 eggs
3 Tbl. water
1 tsp. soy sauce
½ cup chopped water chestnuts
½ cup chopped ham, cooked chicken, turkey or shrimp
    Sesame seeds, optional

In a 1-quart soufflé dish or fairly straight-sided casserole dish, combine the oil, bean sprouts, onions, and celery; sprinkle lightly wth salt and pepper. Cover with wax paper and cook 3 minutes. Meanwhile, beat together eggs, water, soy sauce and additional salt and pepper, if desired, until light and frothy. When vegetables are cooked add water chestnuts, ham, chicken, turkey or shrimp; stir in egg mixture. Cook, covered with wax paper, on full power about 6 minutes or until eggs are set but still soft. After 3 minutes of cooking lift outer edges of the egg mixture to allow the uncooked portion to flow to the outside edges. Sprinkle top with sesame seeds if desired. Let stand a few minutes. Top each serving with BROWN SAUCE; recipe is on page 195.

Makes 4 servings.

FOOD FOR THOUGHT:

I usually combine the ingredients for the sauce in advance. After the casserole has cooked, I cook the sauce (it only takes 3½ minutes). That way it too is piping hot at serving time.

Casserole reheats nicely! If refrigerated, cover with wax paper and microwave on full power 4 to 5 minutes.

Breads

BREADS

Timing is very important in cooking breads, as they cook very rapidly. Overcooking will cause them to become tough, hard and very dry. Remember, breads and cakes will not brown in the microwave oven.

Defrosting of bread products depends on the size and how hard they are frozen. A loaf of bread may be taken directly from the freezer and quickly defrosted. Open the bag, removing the metal twist tie if there is one, and microwave on full power until you can see a drop or two of moisture inside the wrapping. This will take about 1 minute to 1 minute 30 seconds. If you have a defrost setting, it will take 1 minute 30 seconds to 2 minutes. Either way, rotate the package once or twice during the defrosting time.

Dinner rolls will heat quickly also, but should be heated only until slight warmth is felt on the outside. Overheating results in tough or dry rolls. Place rolls on a napkin, paper toweling, or in a wicker basket that is lined with a napkin (make sure the basket does not have a wire reinforcement around the top), and heat 10 to 15 seconds for one roll. Allow approximately 5 seconds for each additional roll.

It will take approximately 20 seconds to defrost and heat a frozen roll. Allow 7 to 10 seconds for each additional roll.

When reheating breads, time for short periods and only until a slight warmth is felt on the surface. Remember, since there is no radiated heat in the microwave oven, surface heat will not be as great as in conventional heating.

Apple Date Puffs

Can be served as breakfast rolls or as dessert when topped with rum sauce.

> ¾ cup (one small) finely chopped apple
> ½ cup finely chopped dates
> 2 Tbl. brown sugar
> 1 Tbl. water

* * * * * * * * * *

> 1 can refrigerated crescent rolls
> Cinnamon

Place apples, dates, sugar and water in a utensil suitable for the microwave oven. Cook covered until apple is tender, about 3 minutes. Set aside to cool slightly. Unroll crescent rolls and spread about 1 Tbl. of the mixture evenly over each. Roll up, starting at the wide end. Tuck ends under, pinching in place to make a bundle. Sprinkle tops of each with cinnamon. Place in a circle on a wax paper-lined dish.

Cook 4 minutes 15 seconds or until no longer doughy. Remove from wax paper and cool on a wire rack for a few minutes. This is important; otherwise they will become soggy on the bottom. Frost with the following:

> ½ cup powdered sugar
> 2 to 3 tsp. milk
> drop of vanilla or rum extract

Mix ingredients together and blend until smooth.

Makes 8 puffs.

To serve as dessert spoon warm RUM SAUCE (recipe on page 201) over each puff.

Anadama Casserole Bread

A slightly sweet, fragrant bread that is good served warm, toasted, or used to make French toast.

⅓	cup yellow cornmeal
1½	cups cold water
1½	tsp. salt
⅓	cup molasses
2	Tbl. butter or margarine
¼	cup warm water
1	package dry yeast
3¼ to 3½	cups flour, unsifted

* * * * * * * * * *

	Round of wax paper and 1 Tbl. cornmeal for bottom of casserole dish
1	tsp. oil
1	tsp. cinnamon
1	Tbl. melted butter or margarine

In a large bowl suitable for the microwave oven, combine cornmeal, water and salt, mixing well. Cook on full power 6 minutes or until mixture boils, stirring once or twice. Add molasses and butter or margarine; cool to lukewarm (about 10 minutes in the refrigerator).

Dissolve yeast in warm water. Stir into lukewarm cornmeal mixture. Stir in one cup of the flour and beat well. Mix in enough of the remaining flour to make a slightly stiff dough.

Place dough in a 2-quart casserole that has been prepared with a round of wax paper on the bottom, sprinkled with 1 Tbl. cornmeal. Rub top of dough with 1 tsp. oil and pat evenly in casserole; sprinkle with cinnamon. Cover casserole (make sure you leave enough room for the bread to rise). Refrigerate overnight.

In the morning, remove from the refrigerator and let rest at room temperature 10 minutes. Microwave uncovered about 11 minutes or until no longer doughy, and a tester comes out clean when inserted in the center. (I use a long bamboo skewer as a tester.)

Turn out immediately onto a wire rack; after 5 minutes remove wax paper and turn right side up. Brush top with melted butter. Let cool further for easier slicing.

If desired, instead of refrigerating, let bread rise at room temperature (about 1½ hours). Microwave uncovered about 9 minutes.

Makes a large loaf.

To make two small loaves, prepare as above. Divide dough in half and place in two round 1-quart casserole dishes. Microwave refrigerated dough about 8 minutes for each loaf.

FOOD FOR THOUGHT:

Because breads baked in the microwave oven do not brown as in a conventional oven, it's a good idea to choose a recipe that produces a dark batter or dough. Or, use a sprinkle-on topping for eye appeal, such as cinnamon, brown sugar and chopped nuts, cinnamon and sugar, date sugar or toasted sesame seeds.

Whole Wheat Caraway Pull-Apart Bread

2¾   cups whole wheat flour
1   tsp. soda
1   tsp. salt
       Buttermilk to make a very soft dough (about 1¾ cups)
1   tsp. oil
1   tsp. caraway seed
       Coarse or regular salt, optional

Mix first three ingredients; add buttermilk and mix until a soft dough is formed. Turn out onto an oiled dish and pat with hands to form a 10-inch circle. Slash top with sharp knife. Brush top with approximately 1 tsp. oil, then sprinkle with caraway seed and salt.

Cook 7 to 8 minutes, rotating halfway through cooking time. Serve hot. Best when pulled apart rather than sliced.

Reheats nicely!

* * * * * * * * * *

Cheddar Shortbread

An easy-to-do pastry!

Delicious cheese-laden shortbread squares or bars to serve as an appetizer or with soup or salads. May be served warm or cold.

Recipe is on page 16.

Cheesy Biscuit Ring

¼   cup butter or margarine
¼   cup grated Parmesan cheese
¼   cup chopped fresh parsley
¼   tsp. garlic salt or ⅛ tsp. garlic powder and ⅛ tsp. salt
1   can refrigerated biscuits

In an 8-inch glass cake dish or a 9-inch glass pie plate melt the butter or margarine (this will take about 30 seconds). Add cheese, parsley and garlic salt; blend well. Spread mixture evenly over bottom of dish, leaving center clear. Place a custard cup or a glass in center of dish. Cut biscuits into quarters and place on top of mixture, forming a ring.

Microwave about 3 minutes to 3 minutes 15 seconds or until no longer doughy. Be careful not to overcook. Remove custard cup or glass and invert onto serving plate. Serve immediately.

Makes 40 small biscuits.

For variation, use 1 tsp. crushed sweet basil and ½ tsp. paprika in place of chopped parsley.

FOOD FOR THOUGHT:
The cheese mixture gives these good eye appeal, after turning out, even though the biscuits are not browned.

Grace's Refrigerator Bran Muffins

½   cup water
¼   cup butter or margarine
1¼ cup Millers Bran, also known as unprocessed bran
      (available at health food stores and most grocery
      stores)
½   cup brown sugar
1   egg
¾   cup buttermilk
1¼ cups flour, unsifted
1¼ tsp. baking soda
¼   tsp. salt
¾   cup chopped dates or raisins or a combination of both

Measure water into a medium-size bowl that is suitable for the microwave. Microwave on full power until water boils (about 2 minutes). Add butter or margarine and bran; stir until butter is melted and bran softened. Beat in sugar and egg. Blend in remaining ingredients, mixing well.

When ready to use, spoon into double paper-lined cups, or you can use triple paper cups alone.

If you do not have a plastic or ceramic muffin utensil, when making more than 2 muffins at a time it is best to arrange them in a circle on a plate (for ease of getting in and out of oven and for rotation), leaving the center free. Sprinkle each with the following topping, using about ½ tsp. per muffin.

Topping:
¼   cup Grape Nuts cereal or chopped nuts
¼   cup brown sugar
1   tsp. cinnamon

Mix well before distributing over top of muffins.

You may store batter, covered, in refrigerator up to 6 weeks. Do not stir prepared batter prior to each use.

Spoon batter into cups, filling ⅔ full for nice rounded tops. Microwave on full power.

For refrigerated batter, microwave:
1 muffin 45 seconds
2 muffins about 1 minute 15 seconds
4 muffins about 2 minutes
6 muffins about 3 minutes 30 seconds

If baking immediately after preparing batter, microwave time will be slightly shorter because of the warmer beginning temperature. Six muffins will then cook in about 2 minutes 30 seconds.

When done, a toothpick should come out clean when inserted in the center.

Makes about 16 muffins.

FOOD FOR THOUGHT:
Lining utensil with double cupcake papers, or using muffin utensils with holes in the bottom of each cup, helps to prevent some of the condensation that forms on the bottom of muffins. Small custard cups or coffee cups make good holders also.

For variation:
Use ½ whole wheat and ½ white flour. And/or add ¼ cup grated unsweetened coconut (available at health food stores).

Pumpkin Bread

         1   cup solid pack canned pumpkin
         2   eggs
        ½   cup granulated sugar
        ½   cup brown sugar, packed
        ⅓   cup oil
         1   tsp. vanilla
         2   cups flour, unsifted
         1   tsp. *each* baking powder and soda
        ½   tsp. salt
         1   tsp. pumpkin pie spice OR ½ tsp. cinnamon,
                  ¼ tsp. ginger, ⅛ tsp. cloves and ⅛ tsp. allspice
        ½   cup chopped nuts

Prepare an 8½ × 4½ × 3½-inch glass loaf dish by lining sides and bottom with wax paper.

In a large bowl beat together the pumpkin, eggs, sugars, oil and vanilla. Stir in flour, baking powder, soda, salt and spice; blend well. (Batter should be fairly stiff.) Fold in nuts. Turn into prepared loaf dish; level top. Sprinkle with the following topping:

         2   Tbl. chopped nuts
         1   Tbl. brown sugar
    ⅛ to ¼   tsp. pumpkin pie spice or cinnamon

Mix together; distribute evenly over top of batter. Microwave on full power 3 minutes, reduce power setting to 50% or medium power; cook approximately 14 minutes or until a tester comes out clean when inserted in the center. Turn out onto a wire rack to cool.

Makes 1 large loaf.

FOOD FOR THOUGHT:

Topping gives good eye appeal!

The reduced power setting is helpful for more even cooking when baking a dense batter and using a loaf dish.

With full power microwave 8 minutes 30 seconds to 9 minutes, rotating the dish 3 times during cooking.

Pies

PIES

Crumb shells cook very rapidly in the microwave, about 1 minute 30 seconds for a 9-inch shell. Regular pastry shells cook well also, having excellent flavor and flakiness.

Always precook the pie shell before adding the filling; this way the bottom crust does not remain doughy. I do not prick the shell before cooking. If I find it is puffing halfway through the cooking time, when I rotate the dish, I will then prick it with a fork in the puffed area. This method helps prevent juices or liquids in the filling from seeping between the crust and dish.

If a double-crusted pie is desired, microwave separately a top, like a large cookie, or cutouts of dough for placing on top of the cooked filling.

Microwave pie shells in glass, ceramic, or specially formulated plastic or paper for microwave oven use.

MORE FOOD FOR THOUGHT:

Since pie shells will not brown, for good appearance and color you can use butter or margarine in place of shortening. Half whole wheat and half white flour add a nice variation in taste, too, or replace 3 Tbl. of the flour with Millers Bran (also known as unprocessed bran). A few drops of yellow food color added to the water before mixing in also aids in appearance. I like to use a beaten egg in place of the water. Whichever way you choose to prepare the crusts, I think you'll like them, along with the ease and speed in which they're cooked.

Chocolate Dream Dessert Pie

         1   cup chocolate chips or a 6-oz. chocolate bar
        20   large or 2 cups miniature marshmallows
        ½   cup milk
         1   cup cream, whipped, or 2 cups frozen whipped top-
                  ping, thawed (one 9 or 10-oz. container)
              Chocolate Crumb Crust, recipe follows

Place chocolate, marshmallows and milk in a 1½-quart suitable utensil. Cook 2 minutes, stir; cook an additional minute or until marshmallows are almost melted. Stir until mixture is thoroughly blended. Chill in the refrigerator about 30 minutes, until well cooled. Fold in whipped cream or topping and turn into prepared crust. Chill at least 4 hours before serving.

Makes 6 to 8 servings.

                    ****

Chocolate Crumb Crust

        1¼   cups fine chocolate wafer or cookie crumbs
        ¼   cup butter or margarine

Place butter or margarine in a medium-size bowl; heat about 30 seconds or until melted. Mix in wafer crumbs. Pat into a 9-inch glass pie plate or an 8-inch-square glass dish. If using a square dish, pat crumb mixture on the bottom only. If desired, cook 1 minute for an extra crisp crust. Cool before filling. Fill with appropriate filling.

FOOD FOR THOUGHT:

For garnish save about 1 Tbl. wafer or cookie crumbs and 3 Tbl. whipped cream. Dollop whipped cream in center of pie and sprinkle a circle of crumbs around it.

18 to 20 (Famous) Chocolate Wafers will make 1¼ cups crumbs. Use your blender or food processor for making them—it's easier!

This dessert freezes well!

Coconut Pecan Pie

1   9-inch baked pie shell
1/3 cup butter or margarine
1/2 cup brown sugar, lightly packed
3   eggs
1/4 tsp. salt
2   tsp. flour
1   cup dark corn syrup
1   cup chopped pecans
1/3 cup grated unsweetened coconut
      (available at health food stores)
      Pecan halves, optional

For Pie Shell:

Prepare pie shell (recipe on page 151) or use a commercially frozen deep dish shell. Place in a glass or ceramic pie plate. Microwave on full power approximately 4 minutes or until no longer doughy. Watch carefully; it can burn. Cool before filling.

For Filling:

Melt butter or margarine in a large bowl suitable for the microwave. Beat in sugar, eggs, salt, flour and syrup. Stir in nuts and coconut; pour mixture into baked pie shell. Decorate with pecan halves if desired. For gentle and more even cooking, cook on 50% power about 12 minutes or until filling is set. Filling will continue to firm up as it cools.

Makes 6 to 7 servings.

FOOD FOR THOUGHT:

Pie can be cooked on full power. Cook 6 minutes 30 seconds or until filling is set, rotating the dish 3 to 4 times during cooking.

Serve pie topped with sweetened whipped cream for a real taste treat!

Lemon Party Pie

A lemon meringue pie topped with whipped cream!

1	9-inch baked pie shell (see page 151)
¼	cup cornstarch
1⅔	cups sugar
⅓	cup lemon juice
1¾	cups water
1	Tbl. grated lemon rind
4	eggs, separated
3	Tbl. sugar
1	carton (9 oz.) frozen whipped topping, thawed, or 2 cups sweetened whipped cream)
	Colored candy shot, optional

Beat together cornstarch, 1⅔ cups sugar, lemon juice, water, lemon rind and egg yolks in a large bowl or utensil suitable for the microwave oven. Stir well; cook 7 to 10 minutes or until mixture boils and thickens. (Stir mixture often to keep the cooked portion mixed with the uncooked portion, and to keep the thickening agent in suspension.)

Pour into baked pie shell. Cool slightly. Beat egg whites until frothy, adding 3 Tbl. sugar gradually, and continue beating until stiff. Spread meringue over filling, sealing edges. Microwave 3 minutes 30 seconds on 80% power or 3 minutes on full power. Cool away from draft.

When pie is cool, cover meringue with whipped topping or sweetened whipped cream; sprinkle with colored candy shot if desired.

Makes 6 to 8 servings.

FOOD FOR THOUGHT:

Refrigerate until serving time, and any leftovers.

Pumpkin Pie

It's so good, why limit it to Thanksgiving?

1	9-inch pastry shell
2	eggs
½	cup granulated sugar
¼	cup brown sugar, packed
1	Tbl. flour
½	tsp. salt
2½	tsp. pumpkin pie spice
2	cups (16-oz. can) solid pack pumpkin
1¼	cups evaporated milk

Pie Shell:

Prepare your favorite pie crust recipe (see page 151), or use a commercially prepared frozen deep dish pie shell. Place in a glass or ceramic pie plate. Cook 4 to 5 minutes or until no longer doughy. Cool slightly.

Filling:

Beat together eggs, sugars, flour, salt, spice, pumpkin and milk. Pour into cooled crust and microwave on full power 10 to 12 minutes or until filling is set. Rotate the pie 3 times to insure even cooking. Remember, filling will firm up further as it cools.

Serve with whipped cream if desired.

Makes 6 to 8 servings.

FOOD FOR THOUGHT:

For more even and delicate cooking, if your unit has variable power, microwave pie 3 minutes on full power, reduce setting to 50% power, and continue cooking for about 16 minutes or until filling is set.

Refrigerate any leftovers!

Dutch Apple Pie

A creamy apple filling!

1   9-inch baked pie shell (I like to use the Press-In-Pie Crust; recipe is on page 152)

Filling:
- ½   cup sugar
- ¼   cup flour
- 1   tsp. cinnamon
- ½   cup sour cream
- 5   cups (about 5 or 6 medium) peeled, sliced apples

Blend together sugar, flour, cinnamon and sour cream. Mix in apple slices, coating well with sour cream mixture. Place in prepared crust and top with the following:

Topping:
- ½   cup Grape Nuts cereal
- ⅓   cup flour
- ⅓   cup brown sugar
- ¼   cup margarine, softened
- ½   tsp. each cinnamon and nutmeg

Mix together Grape Nuts, flour, brown sugar and margarine. Distribute evenly over apples. Sprinkle with cinnamon and nutmeg.

Microwave about 9 minutes, rotating dish halfway through the cooking time. Apples should be tender enough to be pierced with a fork when done.

FOOD FOR THOUGHT:

Grape Nuts help give the topping a crisp or crunchy texture.

French Apple Pie "My Way"

1 9-inch baked pie shell

Filling:

5-6	cups peeled, sliced apples
¾	cup sugar
1	tsp. cinnamon
1	tsp. grated lemon rind, optional
3	Tbl. flour

Topping:

⅓	cup butter or margarine
½	cup brown sugar, packed
½	cup flour
1	cup rolled oats
	Cinnamon to taste (at least ½ tsp.)

Prepare your favorite pie crust recipe, or use a commercially prepared frozen deep dish pie shell. Place in a glass or ceramic pie plate; microwave 4 to 5 minutes or until no longer doughy. Cool slightly; sprinkle bottom of crust evenly with 1 Tbl. of the flour before adding filling.   (This helps keep the crust from becoming soggy.)

Combine sugar, cinnamon, 2 Tbl. flour, and lemon rind. Sprinkle over apples, mixing well to coat. Turn mixture into prepared crust.

For the topping, mix together brown sugar, the ½ cup flour, and oats. Cut in butter or margarine, until mixture resembles coarse meal. Distribute evenly over apples. Sprinkle evenly overall with cinnamon to taste. This not only gives good flavor, but eye appeal and color as well.

Microwave on full power 9-10 minutes, rotating the dish halfway through the cooking time. Apples should pierce easily with a fork when done.

Makes 6 to 8 servings.

Brownie Pie

A rich, easy and delicious dessert!

⅔	cup shortening
1	cup sugar
2	eggs
1	tsp. vanilla
1	cup flour, unsifted
½	cup cocoa
1	tsp. baking powder
½	tsp. salt
¾	cup chocolate chips
½	cup sliced almonds

* * * * * * * * * *

Ice cream or sweetened whipped cream

Melt shortening in a suitable 1½-quart bowl (this will take approximately 2 minutes). Stir in sugar; add eggs and vanilla, beating well. Stir in flour, cocoa, baking powder and salt. Beat until well blended. Pour into a lightly greased 9-inch pie plate, smoothing out top. Sprinkle with chocolate chips, pressing in lightly with finger tips, then sprinkle with almonds.

Microwave covered with wax paper 4 minutes, rotating dish halfway through cooking time. Be careful not to overcook, as pie should be moist! A toothpick will come out clean when inserted in the center.

When cool, serve topped with ice cream or sweetened whipped cream.

Makes 6 to 8 servings.

Paramount Peanut Pie

An interesting, wholesome pie with a not too sweet tasting custard base filling. It's full of down South goodness!

1	9-inch baked pie shell
1	cup brown sugar, packed
1	Tbl. flour
½	tsp. vanilla
4	eggs
1½	cups milk
1	cup chopped, roasted, salted peanuts
	Sweetened whipped cream or whipped topping
	Additional chopped peanuts for garnish, optional

Prepare the crust on page 151 or use a commercially frozen deep dish pie shell as directed on page 142.

In a mixing bowl, combine the brown sugar, flour, vanilla and eggs, beating well. Stir in milk, then peanuts. Pour into baked pie shell. Microwave on full power about 7 minutes or until filling is set, rotating the dish a quarter of a turn three times during cooking. Let cool, then chill. Garnish with whipped cream or topping and additional chopped peanuts, if desired.

Makes 6 to 8 servings.

FOOD FOR THOUGHT:

Refrigerate any leftovers!

Pie Crust

The egg used in this pastry gives it nice color, making it a good choice for microwave cooking. It's almost failure-proof too!

  1   cup flour, unsifted
  ½   tsp. salt
  ⅓   cup butter or margarine
  1   egg

Mix flour and salt together. Cut in butter or margarine until it resembles fine meal. Beat egg and add to flour mixture, mixing until the pastry dough holds together and will form a ball. Roll out on a lightly floured surface and fit loosely into a 9 or 10-inch pie plate or quiche dish. Do not stretch. Flute edge.

Microwave on full power about 4 to 5 minutes or until no longer doughy. Cool; fill to taste.

FOOD FOR THOUGHT:

When using this pastry with a juicy fruit filling, after the shell has been cooked and cooled, sprinkle the bottom evenly with 1 Tbl. flour or fine dry bread crumbs. This will absorb the juices and help keep the crust from becoming soggy.

* * * * * * * * * *

Chocolate Pie Crust

To flour mixture in recipe above add:

  4   tsp. powdered cocoa
  4   tsp. sugar

Beat egg with 1 tsp. vanilla; proceed as above recipe indicates. Fill with appropriate filling.

Press-in-Pie Crust

Makes pastry making easy—a good choice when you're in a hurry. A shortbread flavor!

    ⅓   cup butter or margarine
    1   egg
    1   Tbl. sugar
    1   cup flour, plus 2 Tbl., unsifted

In a glass mixing bowl, soften butter or margarine (it will take about 25 seconds). With a fork beat in egg and sugar. Stir in flour; mix until dough forms a ball. With fingers press dough evenly into a 9-inch glass or ceramic pie plate. Flute edge. Microwave on full power 4 minutes or until no longer doughy. Cool.

Sprinkle bottom of crust evenly with an additional tablespoon of flour or fine dry bread crumbs before adding a juicy filling. This helps keep the crust from becoming soggy.

FOOD FOR THOUGHT:

If desired you may roll this pastry out. Line pie plate, flute, etc.

In microwave cooking, pie crusts should always be prebaked before filling. It's quick and easy with the microwave oven—only 4 to 5 minutes.

For other thoughts on microwave pie shells, see page 142.

Cakes
and
Cookies

CAKES

Cakes bake light and tender and rise high. It is not necessary to grease and flour cake dishes, however I find it beneficial to place a piece of wax paper cut to fit on the bottom of the dish. (Cut several pieces at one time and keep on hand for future use.) The cake then releases easily after inverting; peel paper off while hot.

Round dishes work best, but others can be used with success. My second choice is a 6 x 10-inch glass utility dish, especially when I wish to cut the cake into squares or bars.

Fill cake dishes only half full with batter, and make as level as possible.

* * * * * * * * * *

Cakes are done when a toothpick inserted in the center comes out clean. The cake will also pull away slightly from the sides of the dish. Do not overcook or they will toughen and dry out.

Sometimes a little moisture will remain on top of cakes, but usually disappears while cooling. Touch the moist spot with your finger tip to see if the cake is done beneath before adding more microwave time. If moisture is bothersome, try sprinkling with a little powdered sugar to absorb the excess.

* * * * * * * * * *

If cakes rise unevenly in your microwave, rotate the dish one-fourth turn three times during the microwave time. Opening the oven door will not cause the cake to fall. Elevating the cake dish on another inverted dish or rack while microwaving may also help to insure better cooking.

* * * * * * * * * *

Remember, cakes will not brown, but browning is not missed, as cakes normally are frosted, glazed or sprinkled with powdered sugar.

Let cake stand directly on counter 5 to 10 minutes before turning out onto serving plate, for best results.

Because of the tenderness of microwave cooked cakes, for easier frosting refrigerate cooled cakes for 30 minutes or longer before frosting.

Apricot Brandy Cake

A favorite of mine!

    1   box (9 oz.) yellow cake mix or ½ of a regular size
            box mix (1¾ cups)
    1   egg
    ½   cup water
    ½   cup brandy
    ⅓   cup apricot preserves

    1   carton (9 oz.) frozen whipped topping, thawed
    ¼   cup apricot preserves
    2   Tbl. brandy
    ½   cup toasted almonds

To whipped topping fold in ¼ cup preserves. Set aside in refrigerator. Before using mix in 2 Tbl. brandy to smooth mixture out.

To dry cake mix add egg and water, beating well. Pour half the batter into an 8-inch round glass dish that has a round piece of wax paper on the bottom. Cook 3 minutes 30 seconds. Turn out onto a cake platter. Cook second layer only 3 minutes, as dish is usually warm from cooking first. Turn out onto a wire rack to cool.

While second layer is cooking sprinkle first layer with ¼ cup brandy and spread with ⅓ cup preserves. When second layer is cool place on top of first. Sprinkle with remaining ¼ cup brandy.

Frost cake with whipped topping mixture, using just enough on sides of cake for almonds to stick; spread remaining mixture on top. Stick toasted almonds on sides of cake, saving a few for garnish on the top center. Chill cake well, as long as overnight, before serving.

Makes 6 servings.

FOOD FOR THOUGHT:

To toast almonds, see page 219.

No box mix? Make the SUPER SIMPLE YELLOW CAKE; recipe is on page 166.

Hawaiian Carrot Cake

My daughter Gayl shares this recipe with us.

1	can (20 oz.) crushed pineapple
¾	cup oil
1⅓	cups sugar
1	tsp. vanilla
3	eggs
2½	cups flour, unsifted
1	tsp. salt
1	tsp. baking powder
1	tsp. soda
1	tsp. cinnamon
¾	tsp. ginger
½	tsp. nutmeg
2	cups finely shredded carrots (about 6 medium)
1	cup Angel Flake coconut

Drain pineapple well, reserving ¼ cup for icing. Beat together oil, sugar and vanilla, mixing well. Add eggs, one at a time, beating well after each addition until creamy. Mix together flour, salt, baking powder, soda, cinnamon, ginger and nutmeg. Stir into creamed mixture alternately with carrots and coconut. Fold in all but the ¼ cup reserved pineapple. Turn into a 9-inch bundt dish.

Microwave about 11 minutes on full power, rotating the dish three times during cooking. Let cool in pan. When cool, turn out and frost with following frosting:

Cream 2 Tbl. soft butter, 1½ cups sifted powdered sugar, 1 tsp. grated lemon peel, and ¼ tsp. mace. Stir in the ¼ cup well-drained pineapple.

FOOD FOR THOUGHT:

There are now on the market ceramic, plastic and glass bundt cake dishes that are made for microwave cooking. Some plastics are high heat resistant and can also be used in the conventional oven.

Chocolate Rum Cake

1   chocolate cake mix or your favorite chocolate cake recipe
1   Tbl. cinnamon
½   tsp. cloves
1   carton (9 oz) frozen whipped topping, thawed, OR 2 cups sweetened whipped cream
⅓   cup powdered instant chocolate drink mix
½   cup rum
    Maraschino cherries, for garnish

Prepare cake as directed, adding cinnamon and cloves to ingredients. Make two layers by dividing batter and baking in a 6 × 10-inch glass utility dish or an 8-inch round glass or plastic cake dish. On the bottom of the dish first place a piece of wax paper cut to fit.

Cook each layer approximately 6 minutes on full power or until a toothpick comes out clean. Rotate the dish once or twice during the microwave time if necessary to insure even cooking. (If using the 6 × 10-inch dish, after each layer cools slightly, cut sides and ends off to make straight and even.) Brush or drizzle rum over each layer.

Into the whipped topping or whipped cream fold the powdered chocolate drink mix. Put one-half of the mixture between the layers and the other half on top, leaving sides exposed. Decorate with maraschino cherries. Chill several hours.

This cake freezes well and slices more easily when frozen.

Makes 8 servings.

Lemonade Cheesecake Bundt

The flavor improves if made a day ahead of serving time.

1   package (3 oz.) cream cheese
1   package (18½ oz.) white cake mix
1   cup sour cream
1   can (6 oz.) frozen lemonade concentrate, defrosted
3   eggs

Prepare a ceramic or glass bundt dish by greasing lightly and sprinkling with sugar. Soften the cream cheese by removing the foil wrapper and placing it in a large mixing bowl that is suitable for the microwave. Microwave on full power 10 to 15 seconds. Add dry cake mix, sour cream, lemonade and eggs. With a mixer blend ingredients until moistened, then beat at high speed 4 minutes. Pour into prepared dish, filling ⅔ full and making as level as possible.

Microwave on full power 11 to 12 minutes or until cake tester comes out clean. Rotate the dish three times during cooking. Leave upright until almost cool. (It is normal for cake to fall slightly.)

Invert onto a serving plate; top with following:

1   cup sour cream
¼   cup sugar
¼   tsp. vanilla

Mix together all ingredients; spread on top of cake, allowing some to run down sides. Refrigerate until serving time, and any leftovers.

Makes about 10 servings.

When using this small bundt dish make cupcakes with the remaining batter. Use double cupcake papers in custard cups, coffee cups or a microwave cupcake utensil, filling half full. Microwave 6 cupcakes about 2 minutes.

FOOD FOR THOUGHT:

If you have difficulty removing the cake from the dish, loosen around edges with a knife; microwave a wet towel for 30 to 45 seconds or until hot. Place towel on bottom of inverted dish. Tap lightly after a few seconds and cake should release.

Triple Lemon Bundt

  1   package (18½ oz.) lemon-flavored cake mix
  ½   cup oil
  1   cup water
  4   eggs
  1   package (3⅝ oz.) lemon-flavored gelatin or instant
       pudding mix

Mix all ingredients together, beating well. Pour into a lightly greased ceramic bundt dish that has been sprinkled with sugar. Use all but ½ cup batter. Microwave on full power approximately 10 minutes. If using a plastic bundt dish, microwave on full power about 11 minutes. The plastic bundt is generally larger, and will hold all the batter, thus increasing the cooking time. Let cake cool in dish 10 minutes before inverting onto cake plate. Top with following:

  ½   cup sugar
  2   Tbl. cornstarch
       Dash salt
  1   egg yolk
 1½ tsp. grated lemon peel
  3   Tbl. lemon juice
  1   Tbl. butter
  ⅔   cup water
       Few drops yellow food color, optional
       Flaked coconut, optional

Combine all ingredients, making sure cornstarch is dissolved. Microwave 2 to 4 minutes until mixture boils and thickens. Spoon over cake, letting some run down sides. Top with flaked coconut, if desired.

Makes about 10 servings.

FOOD FOR THOUGHT:

If your unit has variable power you may want to microwave bundt cakes at a slower rate of speed. If so, microwave at 60% power about 16 minutes or until cake tester comes out clean.

Make cupcakes with any leftover batter!

Pumpkin Crème

        1   package (3¼ oz.) vanilla pudding mix, not instant
  1 to 2   Tbl. sugar
        1   tsp. pumpkin pie spice
     1¼   cups milk
        1   cup solid pack canned pumpkin

In a 4-cup suitable utensil combine the pudding mix, sugar and pumpkin pie spice. Stir in milk, blending well. Cook about 5 minutes or until mixture boils, stirring 2 to 3 times during cooking. Mix in pumpkin. Chill, covering with wax paper or plastic wrap. Fill cake layers with mixture or spoon over top of each cake serving. Or spoon into 4 to 6 parfait glasses, alternating with 1 cup whipped cream or topping. Garnish with chopped nuts, if desired.

Small Cakes Using Coeur à la Crème Molds

If you're lucky enough to own these ceramic molds, they make perfect cooking utensils for small heart-shaped cakes at Valentine's Day.

Place a piece of wax paper, cut to fit, on the bottom of the mold for easy cake removal.

Half of an 18½-oz. cake mix makes 8 to 10 cakes. For each cake use 2½ to 3 Tbl. batter. Cook 4 cakes 2 minutes 15 seconds to 2 minutes 30 seconds. Turn out onto a wire cake rack to cool. Frost as desired.

Quick and Easy Coffee Cake

  1   cup flour, unsifted
 ½   cup sugar
  2   tsp. baking powder
       Dash salt
 ½   cup milk
  1   egg
 ½   tsp. vanilla
  3   Tbl. butter or margarine, melted

Beat together all ingredients. Pour batter into an 8 or 9-inch round glass baking dish. Top with following:

 ⅓   cup sugar
  1   tsp. cinnamon
 ¼   cup chopped nuts and ¼ cup Grape Nuts cereal or
       ½ cup of either

Distribute evenly over top of batter. Microwave on full power about 5 minutes 15 seconds or until a toothpick comes out clean. Rotate the dish once or twice during cooking.

FOOD FOR THOUGHT:

Another delicious streusel topping can be made in the following way:

Combine ½ cup flour, ¼ cup butter or margarine, ⅓ cup sugar and 2 tsp. cinnamon. Rub ingredients together with finger tips until butter or margarine is evenly distributed and mixture is crumbly. If desired, add a few finely chopped nuts. Sprinkle evenly over top of batter. Microwave as directed above.

Desserts
and Other
Sweet
Treats

Baked Apples

Choose 4 firm baking apples of medium size. Wash and core. Remove at least one inch of peel from top of each apple. Place apples in a baking dish or in individual custard or dessert dishes. Fill each center with brown or granulated sugar and a dab of butter; sprinkle with cinnamon to taste. Microwave covered with wax paper 5 to 6 minutes or until easily pierced with a fork. Apples will continue to cook slightly after removing from oven.

Makes 4 servings.

For variation or a delightful dessert, try . . .

Rosy Baked Apples

Choose red apples and fill each center ½ to ¾ full with cinnamon red hot candies and a dab of butter if desired. Microwave as above. Serve either warm or cool, plain or with ice cream, whipped cream or table cream.

FOOD FOR THOUGHT:

One medium apple will cook in about 2 minutes 30 seconds. Add one minute cooking time for each additional apple.

For a special taste treat, cut apples in half before cooking; when cool, top with ice cream. Serve half an apple per person.

If filling centers of apples with raisins, dates, or nuts, additional cooking time will be needed for the added ingredients.

Bananas Flambé

A dramatic presentation if flamed at the table in the dark.

¼	cup butter
6	bananas (firm or slightly tipped with green)
¼	cup brown sugar, packed
	Cinnamon to taste
½	cup rum, fruit flavored brandy or liqueur
	Chopped nuts or coconut for garnish, optional

Choose a utensil that is suitable for the microwave, that can withstand the high heat of flaming, and can also be taken to the table for service. I like to use an oval au gratin dish.

Melt the butter (this will take about 30 seconds on full power). Stir in brown sugar and cinnamon to blend. Peel and cut bananas into chunks; add to butter-sugar mixture, stirring gently to coat. Microwave on full power 3 to 4 minutes or until sugar is slightly melted. Remove from microwave oven.

In a glass measure microwave the rum, brandy or liqueur for 30 seconds to warm. Pour over bananas and ignite. When flame dies out, sprinkle with chopped nuts or coconut, if desired. Spoon over scoops of ice cream in dessert dishes. When serving make sure each guest gets some of the delicious syrup.

Makes 12 small servings.

FOOD FOR THOUGHT:

Use caution when flaming!

Only using 4 bananas? Microwave 2 minutes 30 seconds to 3 minutes.

For variation: Instead of serving with ice cream, spoon bananas into dessert dishes and top with sweetened whipped cream.

Peaches Elégante

A delicate dessert or fruit for that special brunch.

    1   can (29 oz.) peach halves or slices
    ⅔   cup apricot-pineapple preserves
    ⅓   cup brandy
    ½   cup coconut

Drain peaches well; arrange in a shallow suitable baking dish. In a small bowl combine preserves and brandy. Spoon over peaches and top with coconut. Heat uncovered in microwave 4 to 5 minutes. Serve warm or cold.

Makes 4 to 6 servings.

When served as dessert, top with ice cream or whipped cream if desired. Heat in stemmed champagne or dessert glasses for an elegant flair.

FOOD FOR THOUGHT:

Do not use lead crystal stemware in the microwave!

Acapulco Apple Crêpes

A Mexican version of the French crêpe. Flour tortillas are substituted, but are they ever good and easy!

GOLDEN APPLE FILLING recipe, page 178,
OR 1 can prepared apple pie filling
8 to 10 small snack-size flour tortillas
Cinnamon to taste
1 recipe RUM SAUCE, page 201
Whipped topping, optional

Spoon apple filling down center of each tortilla and roll up; place seam side down in a glass utility dish or on suitable individual serving plates. Pour rum sauce overall; sprinkle with cinnamon. Heat in microwave until hot through. One will heat in about 1 minute 15 seconds, 4 will take about 4 minutes, and 8 will heat in about 6 minutes 45 seconds.

Garnish with whipped topping before serving, if desired.

Makes 8 to 10 servings.

FOOD FOR THOUGHT:

Tortillas roll easier if warmed first. Place package in microwave or put tortillas between two paper plates; heat 35 to 40 seconds.

177

Golden Apple Filling

A filling rich with flavor that is great for crepes, omelets, or flan.

>   2   Tbl. butter or margarine
>   ½   tsp. grated lemon peel
>   1½   tsp. lemon juice
>   ¼   tsp. nutmeg
>   1   tsp. cinnamon or to taste
>   ¼   cup sugar
>   1   Tbl. flour
>   3   medium (about 3 cups sliced) Golden Delicious apples
>   1   Tbl. brandy or rum, optional

Melt butter or margarine (about 20 seconds) in a utensil suitable for the microwave. Blend in sugar, lemon peel and juice, nutmeg, cinnamon and flour. Peel, core and slice apples in ½-inch slices. Add to sugar mixture; stir to coat.

Cook about 4 minutes 30 seconds or until apples are fork-tender. Stir in brandy or rum, if using.

May be made as far ahead as two days. Keep covered and refrigerated.

* * * * * * * * * *

Apple Date Puffs

An apple-date filling surrounded with a puffy dough; the recipe is on page 133.

Serve topped with warm RUM SAUCE; recipe is on page 201.

Cereal Pineapple Crisp

A tasty variation of a fruit crisp.

    1   cup rolled oats
    ¼   cup Grape Nuts cereal
    ½   cup light brown sugar, packed
    ⅓   cup flour
    ½   tsp. cinnamon
    ½   tsp. ginger
    ⅓   cup butter or margarine, melted

                * * * * * * * * * *

    1   can (16 oz.) crushed pineapple, unsweetened
    1   can (16 oz.) pineapple chunks, unsweetened
    ⅓   cup maraschino cherries, quartered
    ¼   cup rum or pineapple juice
    ¼   cup granulated sugar

Combine oats, Grape Nuts, brown sugar, flour, cinnamon and ginger; add butter and mix well. Set aside.

Drain pineapple, reserving ¼ cup juice if using in place of rum. Combine pineapple, cherries, rum or reserved pineapple juice and sugar in a shallow 1½-quart baking dish. Sprinkle cereal mixture evenly over fruit.

Cook about 12 minutes, rotating dish once or twice. Serve warm or cold, plain or with whipped cream or ice cream.

Makes 8 generous servings.

FOOD FOR THOUGHT:

Serve for breakfast with half and half—delicious!

Since moisture evaporation is minimal in the microwave, the Grape Nuts cereal in this recipe helps give the topping a crisp texture.

Pineapple Jewel Dessert

One of my family's favorites—developed for a low-fat diet.

1	cup flour, unsifted
1	cup sugar
1	tsp. vanilla
1	egg, beaten
¼	tsp. salt
1	tsp. baking soda
1¼	cups crushed pineapple, including syrup

Topping:

½	cup light brown sugar, packed
½	cup Angel Flake coconut

Combine flour, sugar, vanilla, egg, salt, soda, and pineapple; beat well. Spread into an 8 × 8-inch or 6 × 10-inch glass baking dish. Mix together the brown sugar and coconut; spoon over batter, distributing evenly.

Microwave about 8 minutes, rotating the dish 3 times during cooking. Cool; cut into squares. If you can afford the calories, serve topped with whipped cream or ice cream.

FOOD FOR THOUGHT:

Note that there is no oil or shortening in this dessert!

Coconut Custard Dessert

Layers of cake and custard are formed as it cooks. Use lower power setting for delicate cooking.

4	eggs
2	cups milk
½	cup biscuit mix
3	Tbl. butter or margarine
½	cup sugar
1	tsp. vanilla
⅛	tsp. salt
1	cup coconut
	Nutmeg

In a blender place all the ingredients except ¼ cup coconut and nutmeg. Process 15 to 25 seconds; pour into a greased 9-inch glass cake dish or a 10-inch glass or ceramic pie plate. Sprinkle top with the remaining ¼ cup coconut and nutmeg (this gives good eye appeal to the cooked dessert).

Microwave on full power 5 minutes; reduce setting to 50% power and cook 10 to 12 minutes or until a knife comes out clean when inserted near center. Let cool before serving.

Makes 6 servings.

For variation, toast coconut first. Place 1½ Tbl. butter or margarine in a suitable utensil and heat until melted (about 20 seconds). Stir in coconut and microwave about 3 minutes 30 seconds or until toasted to desired degree. Watch carefully so as not to burn it! Let cool before using in above recipe.

If desired, serve dessert topped with sweetened whipped cream.

FOOD FOR THOUGHT:

Fifty percent power is the defrost cycle or medium power setting on many microwave ovens.

Pumpkin Cheesecake

Delightful! A medium power setting is used for this recipe.

Crust:

¾	cup fine gingersnap crumbs (about 18 cookies)
2	Tbl. butter or margarine, softened
1½	Tbl. sugar

Filling:

1	package (8 oz.) cream cheese
⅓	cup sugar
2	Tbl. flour
½	tsp. vanilla
2	eggs
¾	cup solid pack pumpkin
½	tsp. pumpkin pie spice

Topping:

Mix together:

1	cup sour cream
1	tsp. vanilla
2	Tbl. sugar

Combine ingredients for crust, mixing well. Since you cannot use a metal spring form pan in the microwave oven you can make a substitute in the following manner: Place a large piece of wax paper in an 8 or 9-inch round glass cake dish so that the paper extends up the sides of the dish. At various intervals slit the side of the paper down to the bottom of the dish to prevent the paper from crumpling. Place on top of the wax paper 2 (two) paper plates that have been cut to fit the bottom of the dish. Oil the plates lightly.

Pat crumb mixture, reserving 1 Tbl. for garnish, into the bottom of the prepared dish. Microwave 1 minute 30 seconds. Set aside to cool.

In a large bowl soften cream cheese. (Remove foil wrapper; it will take about 30-45 seconds to soften a package taken directly from the refrigerator.) Beat until smooth, then add remaining ingredients, beating well; pour into prepared crust. Microwave on full power 7 minutes. Reduce power setting to 50% and cook 5 minutes longer.

Spread topping on evenly; continue cooking for 3 minutes. Refrigerate at least 4 hours. Lift cheesecake out of the dish with the wax paper extensions. Remove paper carefully and place cheesecake with paper plates onto serving plate. Refrigerate until ready to serve. Just before serving, garnish top with the 1 Tbl. reserved crumbs.

Makes 8 servings.

FOOD FOR THOUGHT:

If you would prefer to make this in a 9-inch glass pie plate, just call it a PUMPKIN CHEESE PIE!

Eliminate the wax paper and paper plates on the bottom of the dish.

Fifty percent power is the medium setting or the defrost cycle on many microwave ovens.

Pumpkin Custard with Ginger Rum Cream

Serve in place of pumpkin pie; especially nice for those who don't care for pie crust.

2	eggs
1	can (16 oz.) solid pack pumpkin
1⅓	cups evaporated milk
1	Tbl. pumpkin pie spice
1	Tbl. flour
½	tsp. salt
½	cup brown sugar, packed
½	cup granulated sugar
3	Tbl. rum

In a large bowl beat eggs well; add remaining ingredients and beat until well blended. Pour into a lightly greased 1½-quart glass casserole or soufflé dish. Cook 3 minutes on full power; reduce setting to 50% power and continue to cook for approximately 14 minutes or until a knife comes out clean when inserted near center. Cool. Serve with GINGER RUM CREAM; recipe follows.

Makes 6 servings.

* * * * * * * * * *

Ginger Rum Cream

1	cup whipping cream
½	tsp. ground ginger
3	Tbl. powdered sugar
3	Tbl. rum

Chill bowl and beaters. Whip cream until almost stiff. Beat in ginger and powdered sugar. Fold in rum. Serve immediately.

Whipped cream may be stabilized if desired. Soften ½ tsp. unflavored gelatin in 1 Tbl. cold water, in a small custard cup or glass measure. Microwave 15 seconds to dissolve; cool. Beat whipping cream until frothy. Gradually add cooled gelatin while beating. Beat until cream piles softly. Add sugar and flavorings; beat until cream stands in peaks when beater is lifted. Refrigerate until ready to use. This will keep nicely for a couple of days!

FOOD FOR THOUGHT:

For simplicity, use 1 carton (9 oz.) frozen whipped topping, thawed. Fold in ½ tsp. ginger and 3 Tbl. rum. Refrigerate until ready to use.

* * * * * * * * * *

To defrost frozen whipped topping in the microwave oven:

Place topping in its plastic container, with lid removed, in the microwave oven. Set power to 50% or defrost; microwave 1 minute to 1 minute 30 seconds, breaking up topping every 15 seconds. Watch carefully as it melts easily; finish defrosting at room temperature for 5 to 10 minutes if necessary.

Pecan 'n' Coconut Squares

Similar to pecan pie!

Crust:

½	cup butter or margarine
3	Tbl. sugar
1	egg
1½	cups flour, unsifted

Melt the butter or margarine in a large bowl that is suitable for the microwave (this will take about 45 seconds). Add sugar and mix well. Beat in egg until well blended. Stir in flour, mixing until a soft dough is formed. Press as evenly as possible into a 6 × 10-inch glass or ceramic dish. Microwave 4 minutes, rotating dish after 2 minutes.

Filling:

1	Tbl. flour
⅔	cup brown sugar, packed
½	cup corn syrup
2	eggs
½	tsp. vanilla
¼	cup coconut
¾	cup chopped pecans

Mix flour and brown sugar together. Add corn syrup, eggs and vanilla; beat until well blended. Stir in coconut and ½ cup of the chopped pecans. Pour over baked crust. Sprinkle with remaining pecans.

Microwave on full power 7 minutes 15 seconds to 8 minutes, or until filling is set. Rotate the dish three times during cooking. For more even cooking use a 50% power setting and cook 13 to 15 minutes. Cool. Cut into squares and serve topped with sweetened whipped cream if desired.

Makes 8 servings, 2½ × 3 inches square.

Black Walnut Fudge

  1   pound powdered sugar
 2/3   cup powdered milk
 1/3   cup light brown sugar, packed
 1/8   tsp. salt
 1/2   cup butter
 1/4   cup milk
 3/4   cup chopped black walnuts

In a 1½-quart deep bowl suitable for the microwave oven combine the sugars, powdered milk, and salt. Place butter on top of mixture and pour milk overall. Cook 3 minutes 30 seconds; stir to blend well. Mix in ½ cup black walnuts. Spread into a lightly oiled 8-inch-square pan. Sprinkle top with remaining ¼ cup nuts and press in lightly. Refrigerate until firm. Cut into 30 pieces.

* * * * * * * * * *

Chocolate Peanut Butter Candy

Similar in taste to a popular candy cup.

  1   cup powdered sugar
 2/3   cup peanut butter
 1/3   cup evaporated milk
 10   large or 1 cup miniature marshmallows
  1   package (6 oz. or 1 cup) chocolate chips
 1/2   cup chopped peanuts, optional

Combine all ingredients in a 1½ to 2-quart bowl suitable for the microwave oven. Microwave 2 minutes 30 seconds or until marshmallows melt. Stir well. Pour into a lightly oiled 8-inch-square pan. Sprinkle with ½ cup chopped peanuts, if desired, pressing in lightly with fingertips. Refrigerate until firm. Cut into one-inch squares.

Makes 64 pieces.

Maple Nut Fudge

     1   pound powdered sugar
    ⅔   cup powdered milk
    ⅛   tsp. salt
    ⅓   cup brown sugar, packed
     6   Tbl. butter or margarine
    ¾   tsp. maple flavoring
    ¼   cup water
    ½   cup (2¼ oz. package) chopped nuts; I prefer pecans

In a 1½-quart deep bowl suitable for the microwave, blend together the sugars, powdered milk and salt. Place the butter or margarine on top of the mixture and pour the water overall. Microwave 3 minutes 30 seconds. Stir well to blend. Stir in maple flavoring and nuts. Spread into a lightly oiled 8-inch-square pan. Refrigerate until firm.

Makes about 36 pieces.

* * * * * * * * * *

Grace's Rocky Road Fudge

     1   pound powdered sugar
    ½   cup cocoa
    ½   cup margarine (one cube)
    ¼   cup milk
     1   tsp. vanilla
     2   cups miniature marshmallows
    ½   cup slivered almonds

Combine sugar and cocoa in a deep bowl that is suitable for the microwave oven. Place cube of margarine on top of mixture and pour milk overall. Microwave 2 minutes. Blend; stir in vanilla and mix well. Fold in marshmallows and almonds. Pour into a lightly oiled 8-inch-square pan. Refrigerate at least 20 minutes before cutting into squares.

Makes about 36 pieces.

Sauces

SAUCES

Sauces many times add that extra special touch to meat, vegetables and desserts. An advantage of the microwave is that since cooking is taking place from all sides at once there is no need to worry about scorching on the bottom as in conventional cooking. You must, however, still stir sauces to keep the thickening agent in suspension and to prevent lumping. They often can be made in the same bowl or utensil you will serve from—another nice feature of the microwave!

If the sauce contains milk it is advisable to use a container or utensil double the size of the amount of milk to be used, since it could boil over. Watch carefully!

FOOD FOR THOUGHT:

A wooden spoon may be left in for mixing and stirring for short periods of cooking time, which is very convenient. Sometimes the wooden spoon will feel warm or hot; this is due to absorbed moisture from washing or oil from cooking which is attracting microwaves. Do not leave wooden spoons in for long cooking periods or they may dry out and crack.

194

Brown Sauce

Serve over meats or eggs for an Oriental flavor.

4	tsp. cornstarch
1	cup water
2 to 3	Tbl. soy sauce
1	tsp. instant granular chicken or beef bouillon

Combine all ingredients in a 1½ to 2-cup suitable utensil. Cook, stirring two to three times, until thick and bubbly. This will take about 3 minutes 30 seconds.

Makes 1⅓ cups.

Serve over Egg Foo Young, meat patties or meatballs. Can also be used as a dipping sauce for ORIENTAL MEATBALLS; recipe is on page 24.

* * * * * * * * * *

Mock Butter Sauce

For calorie watchers!

1½	tsp. cornstarch
1	tsp. imitation butter-flavored salt
⅛	tsp. white pepper
½	tsp. dried parsley flakes or 1 Tbl. fresh chopped parsley
½	cup water

Blend together dry ingredients. Add water; stir well. Cook 2 minutes 30 seconds, until clear and thickened. Stir two to three times during cooking. Serve hot over cooked vegetables or fish.

Makes ½ cup.

Celery Sauce

A tasty sauce for fish or green peas.

2 Tbl. butter or margarine
1 cup chopped celery
¼ of a small onion, chopped
½ cup cream or milk
½ tsp. salt
¼ tsp. white pepper
¼ tsp. thyme
   Dash nutmeg, optional
2 Tbl. flour

Place all ingredients in a blender or food processor; process until pureed. Pour into a small cooking utensil or gravy boat that is suitable for the microwave oven. Cook 3 minutes to 3 minutes 30 seconds or until thickened, stirring periodically.

Makes 1 cup.

FOOD FOR THOUGHT:

Watching calories?

Omit butter and salt; substitute 1 tsp. imitation butter-flavored salt.

* * * * * * * * * *

To make CELERY SOUP increase milk to 1 cup; cook 30 to 45 seconds longer.

Makes 2 servings.

Piquant Pimiento Cream Cheese Sauce

A sauce with excellent flavor, yet simplicity.

- 1   package (3 oz.) pimiento cream cheese
- 1   Tbl. lemon juice
- ½   tsp. salt
- ⅛   tsp. garlic powder
- ¼   tsp. onion powder
- 3   Tbl. milk or water

Soften cream cheese in a small utensil that is suitable for the microwave oven. Cream until smooth. Blend in lemon juice, salt, garlic, and onion powders, milk or water. Cook 1 minute 30 seconds.

Stir and serve over hot cooked vegetables.

FOOD FOR THOUGHT:

Always remove foil from cream cheese before placing in the microwave oven or arcing will occur.

It will take approximately 15 seconds to soften a 3-ounce package; 30 seconds for an 8-ounce package.

Sweet~Sour Sauce I

Use as a dipping sauce for Oriental Meatballs or egg rolls.

         1   Tbl. cornstarch
         3   Tbl. cider vinegar
        ½   cup orange juice, pineapple juice or marmalade
        ½   cup brown sugar
        ¼   tsp. ground ginger
         1   Tbl. catsup, optional
         1   Tbl. soy sauce

Combine all ingredients in a two-cup suitable utensil, blending well. Cook until mixture comes to a full boil and is thickened (this will take about 2 minutes). Stir mixture two to three times during cooking. Serve as a dipping sauce or over meatballs, fish or poultry.

Makes about ⅔ cup.

*** *** *** ***

Sweet~Sour Sauce II

Another version for chicken, pork or meatballs.

         4   Tbl. brown sugar
         3   Tbl. cider vinegar
         2   Tbl. cornstarch
        ½   tsp. ground ginger
         1   tsp. salt
         1   can (16 oz.) stewed tomatoes, broken up
         1   can (8 oz.) crushed pineapple

Combine all ingredients in a suitable utensil; mix well. Cook 10 minutes or until mixture comes to a boil and is thickened. Stir mixture after 4 minutes, then every two minutes.

Pour over cooked meat or poultry; reheat and serve.

Makes about 1⅔ cups.

198

Caramel Sauce

Serve warm or cold over ice cream or baked apples. Good as a dipping sauce for fresh apple wedges, banana chunks, marshmallows or pecan halves.

½ cup light brown sugar, packed
¼ cup granulated sugar
¼ cup light corn syrup
3 Tbl. water
2 tsp. butter

In a 2-cup suitable utensil (a glass measuring cup is a good choice) combine sugars, corn syrup and water. Cook 3 minutes to 3 minutes 30 seconds, until sugar is dissolved and mixture comes to a full rolling boil. Stir two to three times during cooking. Add butter; stir until melted. Let cool slightly before serving.

Makes ¾ cup.

FOOD FOR THOUGHT:

For variation: Reduce water to 2 Tbl.; stir in 2 Tbl. rum after stirring in butter.

Or, if a light caramel sauce is desired, after sauce has cooled at least 5 minutes gradually stir in 2 Tbl. cream.

Sauce will be of a thicker consistency when cooled to room temperature or when refrigerated.

Cranberry Sauce

    1½   cups fresh cranberries
    ½   cup sugar
    ¼   cup water

Wash and pick over cranberries and drain well. In a 1-quart casserole or suitable utensil combine ingredients. Cook covered about 5 minutes or until berries pop. Stir once or twice during cooking. Pour into a lightly greased 2-cup mold if desired; refrigerate. Unmold when firm and set.

Makes 2 cups.

For variation use orange juice in place of water and add 1 Tbl. grated orange peel.

The addition of grated orange peel alone is also good.

* * * * * * * * * *

No-Egg Lemon Dessert Sauce

Serve over warm gingerbread squares or holiday plum pudding.

    ½   cup sugar
    1½   Tbl. cornstarch
  2 to 3   Tbl. lemon juice
    1   Tbl. butter
    1   tsp. grated lemon rind
    1   cup water

Combine all ingredients in a suitable utensil and cook about 2 minutes 30 seconds or until mixture comes to a boil and is thickened. Stir once or twice during cooking.

Makes 1½ cups.

FOOD FOR THOUGHT:

One fresh lemon yields about 3 Tbl. juice.

Rum Sauce

A slightly sweet and mellow dessert sauce!

½	cup sugar
2	Tbl. cornstarch
¼	tsp. salt
1½	cups milk
¼	cup butter or margarine
⅛	tsp. mace or nutmeg
½	cup rum

In a large utensil, at least 4-cup capacity, combine sugar, corn-starch and salt. Gradually stir in milk. Add butter or margarine. Cook 6 minutes, stirring occasionally or until sauce is thickened. Stir in rum and serve.

Makes about 2½ cups.

Delicious over Apple Pie, Stewed Apples or use with ACAPULCO APPLE CRÊPES; recipe is on page 177.

Need only half a recipe? Cook 2 minutes 30 seconds to 2 minutes 45 seconds.

This keeps well two to three days in the refrigerator and reheats nicely.

Vegetable Cream Sauce

          2   Tbl. butter or margarine
          2   Tbl. flour
     1½   tsp. dry mustard
       ½   tsp. salt
       ⅛   tsp. white pepper
       ⅛   tsp. garlic powder or 1 clove garlic, finely minced
          1   tsp. Worcestershire sauce
          1   cup milk
       ½   cup sour cream

In a utensil that has at least a 2-cup capacity, and that is suitable for the microwave, melt the butter or margarine (this will take about 20 seconds). Stir in flour, mustard, salt, pepper, garlic, Worcestershire sauce and milk. Cook on full power about 4 minutes or until thick and bubbly, stirring frequently. Stir in sour cream and serve over hot cooked vegetables or potatoes.

Makes 1½ cups.

For variation:

Add a little dill weed, curry powder or horseradish. Or use it as a base for a cheese sauce; stir in ½ cup grated cheese in place of the sour cream.

FOOD FOR THOUGHT:

This is also an excellent sauce over cooked fish.

Jams
and
Jellies

JAMS and JELLIES

The amount of jam or jelly that can be made at one time is limited, but since it is done so rapidly and easily it is not an inconvenience to do several small batches.

Make sure your cooking utensil is large enough, as jams and jellies boil up very rapidly. Boiling will stop immediately when the microwave time is interrupted, or if you have a variable power feature you can reduce the power setting to keep the mixture just under a boil-over level.

Test jelly in the same manner as in conventional cooking. One way is to dip a large metal spoon into the boiling syrup. It should sheet the spoon and drop off in distinct drops rather than flow in a thin stream. Do not use a conventional candy or jelly thermometer in the microwave.

If sealing with paraffin, be aware that paraffin will not melt in the microwave, because it contains no moisture. Also, paraffin seals do not always prevent spoilage, especially in hot, dusty or humid areas. If storing for long periods of time it is best to use glass jars that can be sealed airtight. Fill clean hot jars within ⅛-inch of tops, prepare lids according to manufacturer's directions.

To heat jars, fill half full with water; microwave until water comes to a full boil.

The following recipes are great for small families or for last-minute gift giving.

Apricot Rum Jelly

A subtle flavor of rum makes this unusual.

1½	cups (12 oz.) apricot nectar
1	Tbl. lemon juice
2½	Tbl. powdered jam and jelly pectin
2	cups sugar
¼	cup rum

Combine apricot nectar, lemon juice and pectin in a bowl suitable for the microwave oven, with at least 1½-quart capacity. Bring mixture to a full boil (this will take 5 to 6 minutes). Stir in sugar and bring to a boil again and boil hard for 2 minutes (this will take approximately 6 minutes 30 seconds total cooking time). Skim off foam and stir in rum. Pour into hot sterilized containers. Seal if desired, or keep refrigerated.

Makes about 2 cups.

Cranberry Jelly

An excellent jelly with beautiful color.

      1½   cups cranberry juice cocktail drink
      2   Tbl. lemon juice
      2½   Tbl. powdered jam and jelly pectin
      1½   cups sugar

Combine cranberry juice, lemon juice and pectin in a suitable utensil of at least 1½-quart capacity. Bring to a full boil (about 5 minutes 30 seconds). Stir in sugar, bring to a boil again, and boil hard 2 minutes. This will take approximately 6 minutes 30 seconds total. Skim if necessary and pour at once into sterilized hot containers. Seal if desired, or keep refrigerated.

Makes 3 half-pints.

* * * * * * * * * *

Port Wine Jelly

Similar to the familiar grape jelly, but with a more intriguing taste.

Substitute 1½ cups port wine for the cranberry juice cocktail in the recipe above; proceed as directed.

FOOD FOR THOUGHT:
Either of these jellies makes a nice gift for the holidays!

Strawberry Jam

Delicious and especially easy to make in the microwave.

    1   package (10 oz.) frozen sliced strawberries
    1   Tbl. powdered jam and jelly pectin
    1   cup sugar

In a 1½-quart bowl or utensil suitable for the microwave oven defrost strawberries on full power about 1 minute 30 seconds, or on 50% power or defrost setting for about 4 minutes. Mix together the defrosted strawberries and pectin. Microwave on full power until mixture comes to a full boil (this will take about 3 minutes 30 seconds). Add sugar; stir well. Bring mixture to a full rolling boil and cook 6 to 8 minutes, stirring two to three times during cooking. This will take approximately 8 to 9 minutes total after adding sugar. If your unit has variable power, reduce the power setting to keep the mixture just below a boil-over point. Skim; let cool slightly, mix again, and pour into hot sterilized containers and seal or store in the refrigerator in a covered container.

Makes 1¼ cups.

To use fresh strawberries, wash and hull 2 cups fresh berries (1 pint). Crush berries and stir in pectin; proceed as above, increasing sugar to 1¼ to 1½ cups.

                    * * * * * * * * * *

Red Raspberry Preserves

My favorite! Has a true fruit flavor.

Substitute red raspberries in above recipe and increase sugar to 1¼ cups. Proceed as directed above.

Red Pepper Jam

A spicy appetizer spread or meat embellishment!

1	medium-large red bell pepper to equal 1 cup coarsely chopped
½	cup white vinegar
1½ to 2	Tbl. crushed dried red chili pepper
2	Tbl. powdered jam and jelly pectin
1¼	cups sugar

In a blender, whirl crushed chili pepper for a few seconds; add pepper and vinegar. Blend until pureed. You should now have 1 cup puree. In a large utensil suitable for the microwave oven, about 1½-quart capacity, stir together the puree and pectin. Bring to a full boil (this will take about 3 minutes 30 seconds). Add the sugar, stirring well; bring to another full rolling boil (about 3 minutes). Boil 3 to 5 minutes, stirring periodically. Or you may reduce the power setting to prevent boil-over while still boiling gently, if your microwave oven is a variable power model. Pour into sterilized jars and seal if you plan to store for a long period of time, or keep refrigerated in a covered container.

Makes about 1½ cups.

Serve as an appetizer by spreading a cracker with cream cheese and topping with the jam, or serve as a meat accompaniment to pork, lamb or poultry.

FOOD FOR THOUGHT:

If a red bell pepper is not available, substitute a green pepper and use a couple of drops of red food coloring, if desired.

A large cooking utensil is necessary when making jams or jellies so that the mixture will have room to boil up.

Sherried Peaches

A nice accompaniment for poultry, pork or ham.

1 large can (29 oz.) peach halves or slices, well drained
   (reserve ¼ cup syrup)
½ cup light brown sugar, packed
1 Tbl. finely minced crystallized ginger or ¼ tsp.
   ground ginger
¼ tsp. cinnamon
⅛ tsp. cloves
½ cup dry sherry
1 Tbl. vinegar

In a suitable utensil, such as a glass measuring cup, combine the reserved ¼ cup syrup and the remaining ingredients except peaches. Microwave until sugar is dissolved, about 1 minute 30 seconds. Place peaches in a container and pour syrup over them.

Cover and chill overnight or several days before serving.

Cranberry Chutney I

An exotic accompaniment to curries, poultry, ham or pork.

2	cups fresh cranberries
⅔	cup water
¼	cup white vinegar
½	cup brown sugar, packed
½	cup granulated sugar
½	cup chopped onion
½	cup each raisins and chopped dates
1	clove garlic, minced
1	tsp. cinnamon
¼	tsp. cloves
½	tsp. salt
⅛ to ¼	tsp. cayenne
3	Tbl. finely diced crystallized ginger

Wash and pick over cranberries; drain well. In a 2-quart casserole or other suitable utensil mix together all ingredients. Microwave covered about 17 minutes, or until cranberries have popped. Stir two to three times during cooking.

Pour into hot sterilized jars and seal, or keep refrigerated in a covered container. May be served either warm or cold.

Makes about 3 cups.

Cranberry Chutney II

This version uses canned cranberry sauce!

¼	cup water
¼	cup white vinegar
½	cup brown sugar, packed
½	cup chopped onion
½	cup each raisins and chopped dates
1	clove garlic, minced
1	tsp. cinnamon
¼	tsp. cloves
½	tsp. salt
⅛ to ¼	tsp. cayenne
3	Tbl. finely diced crystallized ginger
1	can (2 cups) whole cranberry sauce

In a casserole or bowl suitable for the microwave, of 1½-quart capacity, mix all ingredients except the cranberry sauce. Cook 8 minutes, stirring once or twice during cooking. Stir in cranberry sauce; cook an additional 5 minutes.

Pour into hot sterilized jars and seal, or keep refrigerated in a covered container. May be served either warm or cold.

Makes about 3 cups.

More Food
For Thought

More Food for Thought

In planning your meal for cooking in the microwave your thoughts should be on the preparation and timing of the food. Think about each recipe and how long it is going to take to cook.

Start with the dish that requires the longest to cook and follow it with others, keeping in mind that some foods retain their heat for quite a while, or will reheat perfectly in the microwave. Leave items that require a short heating or cooking time, such as breads and rolls, for the last!

Because of the speed in which the microwave cooks you may want to set the table prior to starting your meal preparation—of course, you may fit this chore into the time that your food is cooking.

By proper planning and sequencing of food preparation (the order in which you are going to do things) you should have no trouble getting your meal on the table hot.

Your first attempts at microwave cooking a full meal may result in confusion, but soon you will acquire a skilled routine that will give you confidence and the joy of owning a microwave!

As stated in the introduction, beginning food temperature, density, and mass or volume of food will affect the cooking times. When doubling a recipe or amount of food you do not necessarily double the cooking time.

A good rule of thumb is to increase the cooking time by approximately one-third of the single item microwave time. An example: one medium-size potato will cook in about 5 minutes, two will cook in about 7 minutes, three in 9 minutes, and so on. Realize that each person's conception of medium size will vary, along with moisture content of each potato.

Larger potatoes will take longer to cook and smaller potatoes a shorter time. Basically, the more food you add to the oven, the more time it will take to cook. By the way, don't forget to pierce the potatoes before cooking or they could burst from steam buildup.

Most cooks are interested in converting their favorite recipes to microwave cooking. A general rule of thumb is to time for one-fourth of the conventional cooking time, remembering to consider density, beginning temperature of ingredients involved, and mass or volume. Denser items will take longer to cook, as will extremely cold ingredients. Also, additional cooking time is needed when you add more volume to the oven. If a casserole is to bake for one hour conventionally, it will cook in approximately 15 minutes in the microwave. Since it is always best to undercook, check for doneness after 12 minutes of cooking time; however, it could take 17 minutes or longer.

Because evaporation is minimal in microwave cooking, it is sometimes necessary to reduce liquids slightly. For example, if one cup of liquid is called for in a regular recipe, try reducing it to ¾ cup in the microwave adaptation. However, if uncooked rice or pasta is being prepared, the regular amount of liquid is still necessary for rehydration or for the rice or pasta to become tender.

Since there is no dry or radiated heat involved in microwave cooking, food will not get crisp. Evaporation of liquids is minimal, and because of the speed with which some foods cook, they will not brown.

If a crisp texture or further browning of foods is desired, you can place the item under a conventional broiler for a few minutes. Make sure the cooking utensil can withstand the high broiler heat! Also, adjust the microwave cooking time to allow for further cooking from the applied broiler heat. "My Way" to achieve texture, flavor and eye appeal is to use one or two of the following off-the-shelf items.

BRUSH-ONS such as Gravy Master, Kitchen Bouquet, soy sauce or other browning sauces or agents.

SPRINKLE-ONS include dry onion soup mix, dry brown gravy mix, and my favorite, paprika. Cinnamon, nutmeg or brown sugar can also be used.

CRISPY TOPPINGS can be achieved by using chopped nuts, crushed crackers, dry bread crumbs, crushed pretzels, Grape Nuts cereal, or any other crushed dry cereal.

Brown sugar or whole wheat flour in some recipes helps give good color.

Use your imagination and you'll be surprised at how many items there are available to get the result you're after. Eye appeal is important in food presentation, so be creative!

It should be noted that most meats and poultry will start to brown naturally when cooked over 12 to 15 minutes, because of the fat content, the heat generated, and the length of cooking time involved.

With dial timers, when timing for short periods under one minute, get in the habit of turning your timer beyond the 2-minute mark, then back to the actual cooking time desired. The result is more accurate timing, and it takes only a flick of the wrist!

If items are of irregular shape or size, rotating or rearranging can be important for even cooking or more satisfactory results. During cooking it is sometimes necessary to rotate the dish a quarter or half turn or to rearrange the food itself. Many foods require stirring to mix the uncooked portion with the cooked portion, as in conventional cooking.

Use paper toweling to cover items such as bacon, roasts, etc. It is porous, allowing steam to escape, yet absorbs grease and moisture. Helps eliminate oven cleanup too!

Cover with wax paper to keep in a little moisture and heat, along with keeping spatters off the oven walls. Also, wax paper will not absorb toppings or sauces that are on some foods.

Plastic wrap keeps in moisture, for a steamed effect. Or, of course, you can always use the lid to your casserole dish. When using plastic wrap in place of a lid do not stretch tightly. Allow room for the steam to form. If you fail to do so, the plastic wrap may burst. It is advisable not to completely encase a cooking utensil in plastic wrap while cooking.

You no longer truly have leftovers, as they taste like fresh cooked when reheated in the microwave oven. A plate of food will heat in about 2 minutes 30 seconds to 3 minutes. It's nice when members of a family eat at different times!

When reheating foods do not overheat. Heat only until the food is hot. Foods with high sugar or fat content heat very quickly.

Keep your microwave oven interior clean, as spills can add to cooking time. Also, if spills are allowed to build up on the door seal, microwave leakage is possible. Since spatters and spills don't cook on, they wipe up easily with a damp sponge or cloth. What a time-saver!

Be aware that some products have microwave cooking instructions on their package. Also, many magazines now feature microwave recipes.

It should be noted that most of the recipes in this book cook on high or full power. I have inserted a few recipes with variable power cooking and it will be indicated when used. If your unit has the variable power feature it gives you the option at any time to use it as you would your conventional range, allowing sufficient time for slower cooking speed. Each microwave oven manufacturer uses different terminology and often different power levels for the same setting, making it difficult to give you variable power timing for recipes in a general microwave cookbook as this.

Personal preference is still most important! So adjust cooking times and seasonings to your satisfaction.

Microwave Tidbits

It's always best to undercook foods, as overcooking cannot be undone. If additional cooking time is needed add only seconds or a few minutes at a time.

Cheese melts rapidly and becomes tough if overcooked. Add on top of casseroles towards the last part or at the end of the cooking time. For melting, consider using a lower power setting if your microwave is a variable power model.

Melt chocolate or butter easily in the microwave. Using a paper cup for the job eliminates dishwashing!

Soften butter in seconds for creaming or spreading. One-half cup on full power will take 10 to 20 seconds; on 10% power, 1 minute 30 seconds to 2 minutes.

Heat syrup for pancakes or waffles!

Cereals tend to boil over, so it is important that they be prepared in a large enough utensil. Stir several times during cooking to prevent lumping.

Plump raisins by sprinkling with 1 or 2 Tbl. water; microwave on full power 1 to 2 minutes. Stir and let stand a few minutes.

To toast almonds, spread ½ cup sliced or slivered almonds on a paper plate or pie plate. Microwave on full power 6 to 8 minutes, stirring frequently. The time will vary according to freshness of nuts. Watch carefully so they do not burn!

Dry your own herbs: 1 cup of leaves on paper toweling will dry in about 4 minutes. Crush and store in an airtight container.

Toppings such as dry bread crumbs should be added to casseroles after cooking to retain their crispness.

Canapes with a cracker or toast base will have less tendency to become soggy if heated on a paper towel-lined plate. The paper absorbs some of the excess moisture that is formed between the canape and the plate. The same principle applies to reheating waffles, pancakes, French toast and pizza.

Wooden spoons may be left in sauces, puddings, etc., for short periods of cooking time, which makes them convenient for stirring.

Need dry bread crumbs? Place bread slices on paper toweling. Microwave 1 minute 30 seconds to 2 minutes for 1 slice. Time depends on type and freshness or moisture content of bread. When dried, crush with rolling pin or whirl in your blender or food processor.

Croutons may also be made in the same way. Four cups of fresh bread cubes will be dried in about 7 minutes. Stir every 2 minutes during the microwave time.

For a hot compress, it's easier to wring out a cold wet towel than a hot one. Heat a wet towel in the microwave oven for approximately 1 minute; place carefully on those aches or pains!

What Does It Mean?

BLEND—to mix two or more ingredients thoroughly.

CHOP—cut into small pieces.

DICE—cut into small cubes of uniform size.

MINCE—to chop into very fine pieces.

MIX—to combine in any manner so that all ingredients are evenly distributed.

SLIVER—to cut into long, even, thin strips.

STIR—to blend ingredients by mixing together in a circular motion.

It's Nice To Know That

4 ounces of CHEESE equals 1 cup shredded.

2 whole CHICKEN BREASTS (10 ounces each) makes 1½ cups to 2 cups diced.

An average LEMON yields about 3 Tbl. juice and about 3 tsp. grated lemon peel.

1 cup miniature MARSHMALLOWS equals 10 large.

8 medium-size fresh MUSHROOMS equal approximately ¼ pound; 1 pound will make about 4 servings. Sliced, 3 ounces yield about 1 cup.

1 pound of ONIONS equals 3 large. 1 small ONION yields ½ cup chopped.

Three medium-size POTATOES equal approximately one pound, and one pound will make about 4 servings mashed. One pound yields approximately 2½ cups cubed or sliced.

One cup raw RICE yields 3 cups cooked rice.
1 cup QUICK-COOKING RICE yields 2 cups cooked rice.

One pound uncooked SPAGHETTI makes 6 to 8 servings cooked; allow ¾ to 1 cup sauce per serving.

One pound granulated SUGAR equals 2¼ cups.

BROWN SUGAR taken directly from a one-pound package equals 3⅓ cups. Packed, one pound equals 2¼ cups.

1 cup WHIPPING CREAM yields 2 cups whipped.

Index

INDEX

◦§ §◦

Cookbooks by Rand Editions/Tofua Press

MICROWAVE COOKING MY WAY: It's a Matter of Time,
by Grace Wheeler, $8.95
(Calif. tax .54 per book; shipping 1.30 per book)

1E ELEGANT HORS D'OEUVRE, A Collection of Hors d'Oeuvre
Recipes for Conventional and Microwave Cooking
by Margon Edney and Ede Grimm, $5.95
(Calif. tax .36 per book; shipping .95 for 1-2 books)

FOOD WITH A FLAIR: Special Recipes for Special People,
by Doone Lewis, $4.95
(Calif. tax .30 per book; shipping .95 for 1-2 books)

A TASTE OF MEXICO, A Primer of Mexican Cooking,
by Esther Gonzales Davis, $3.95
(Calif. tax .24 per book; shipping .95 for 1-2 books)

DINNER IN THE MORNING,
A Collection of Breakfast and Brunch Recipes,
by Elizabeth N. Shor, $3.95
(Calif. tax .24 per book; shipping .95 for 1-2 books)

Master Charge or Visa accepted;
include card number and expiration date.

To order more copies of

MICROWAVE COOKING MY WAY

Enclose a check for $8.95 for each copy plus $1.30 shipping for
1 book (add .30 shipping each additional book), payable to
Rand Editions/Tofua Press.

California residents add .54 tax per book.

Please send _____ copies of **MICROWAVE COOKING MY WAY** to:

Name _____

Address _____

_____

I enclose a check for _____ (including tax if applicable)
Please charge my _____ Master charge _____ Visa
Card number_____
Expiration date_____

RAND EDITIONS/TOFUA PRESS
10457-F Roselle St., San Diego, CA 92121   (714) 453-4774

To order more copies of

MICROWAVE COOKING MY WAY

Enclose a check for $8.95 for each copy plus $1.30 shipping for
1 book (add .30 shipping each additional book), payable to
Rand Editions/Tofua Press.

California residents add .54 tax per book.

send _____ copies of **MICROWAVE COOKING MY WAY** to:

Name _____

Address _____

_____

I enclose a check for _____ (including tax if applicable)
Please charge my _____ Master charge _____ Visa
Card number_____
Expiration date_____

RAND EDITIONS/TOFUA PRESS
10457-F Roselle St., San Diego, CA 92121   (714) 453-4774

To order more copies of

MICROWAVE COOKING MY WAY

Enclose a check for $8.95 for each copy plus $1.30 shipping for
1 book (add .30 shipping each additional book), payable to
Rand Editions/Tofua Press.

California residents add .54 tax per book.

Please send _____ copies of **MICROWAVE COOKING MY WAY** to:

Name _____

Address _____

_____

I enclose a check for _____ (including tax if applicable)
Please charge my _____ Master charge _____ Visa
Card number_____
Expiration date_____

RAND EDITIONS/TOFUA PRESS
10457-F Roselle St., San Diego, CA 92121   (714) 453-4774

To order more copies of

MICROWAVE COOKING MY WAY

Enclose a check for $8.95 for each copy plus $1.30 shipping for
1 book (add .30 shipping each additional book), payable to
Rand Editions/Tofua Press.

California residents add .54 tax per book.

Please send _____ copies of **MICROWAVE COOKING MY WAY** to:

Name _____

Address _____

_____

I enclose a check for _____ (including tax if applicable)
Please charge my _____ Master charge _____ Visa
Card number_____
Expiration date_____

RAND EDITIONS/TOFUA PRESS
10457-F Roselle St., San Diego, CA 92121   (714) 453-4774